ACOUSTIC GUITAR CHORDS

MADE EASY

by William Bay

MB22088

LARGE PRINT EDITION

Visit us on the Web at www.melbay.com or billsmusicshelf.com

Table of Contents

Table of Contents

How to Read Chord Diagrams

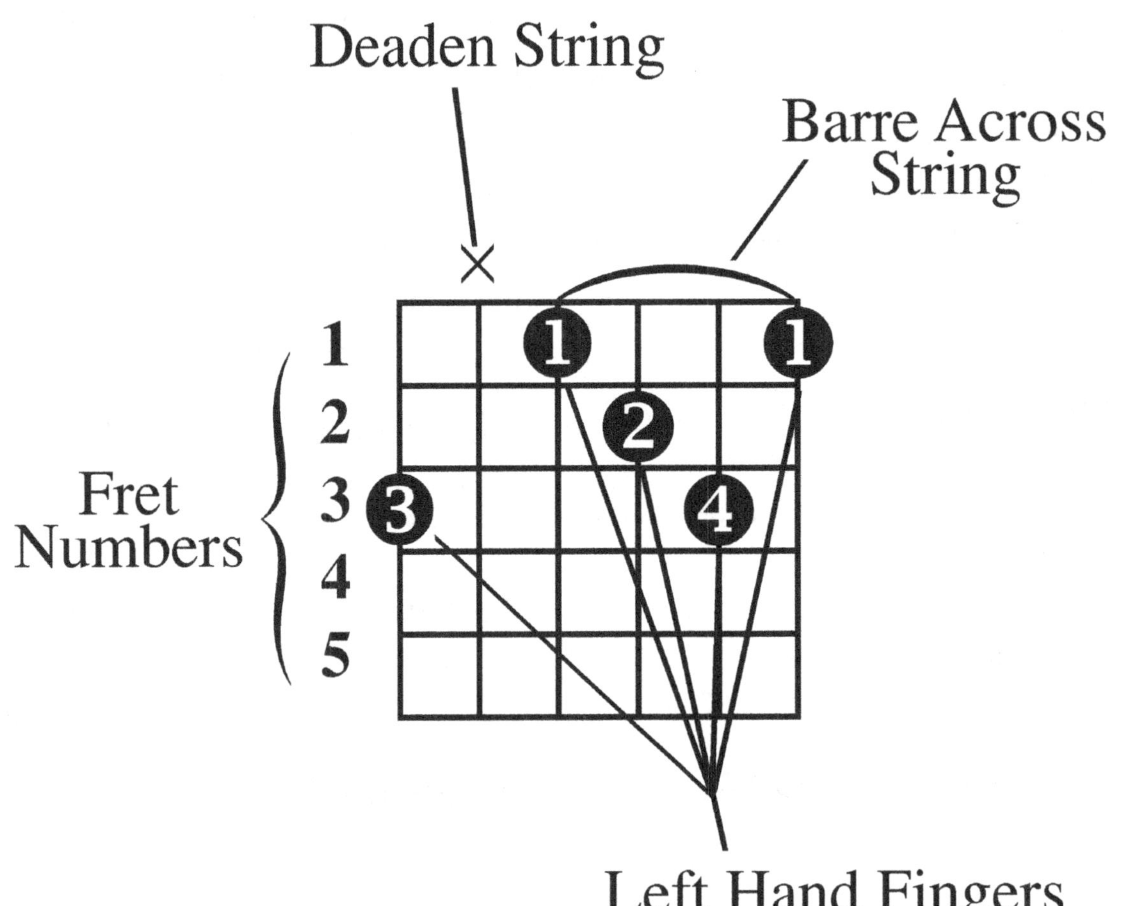

CMajor

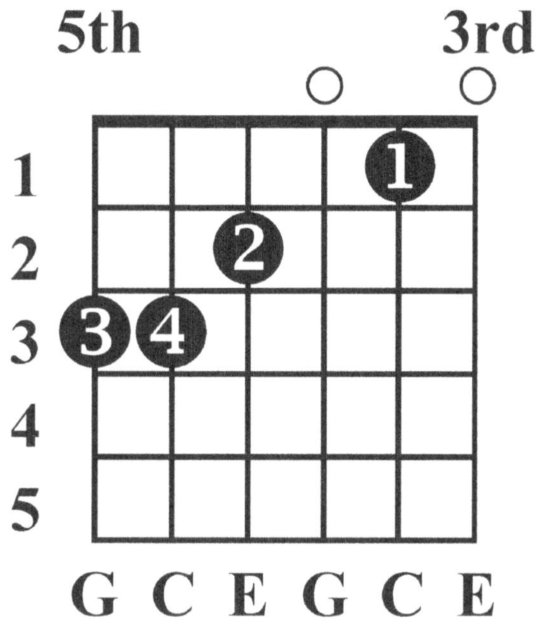

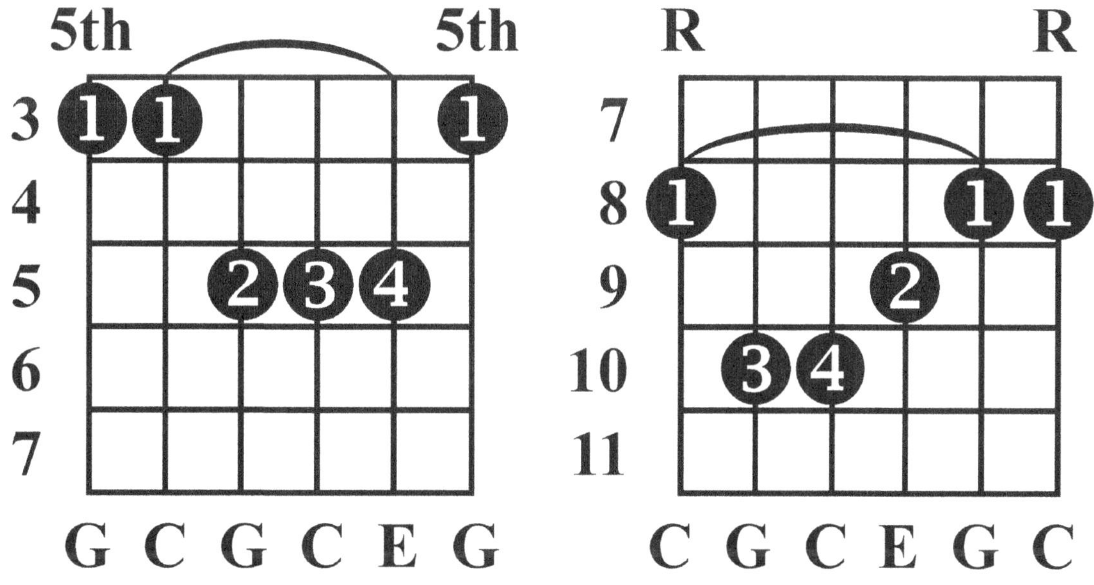

GMajor

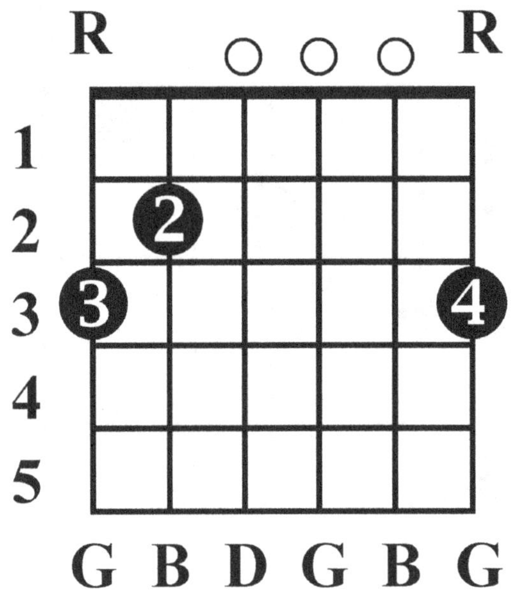

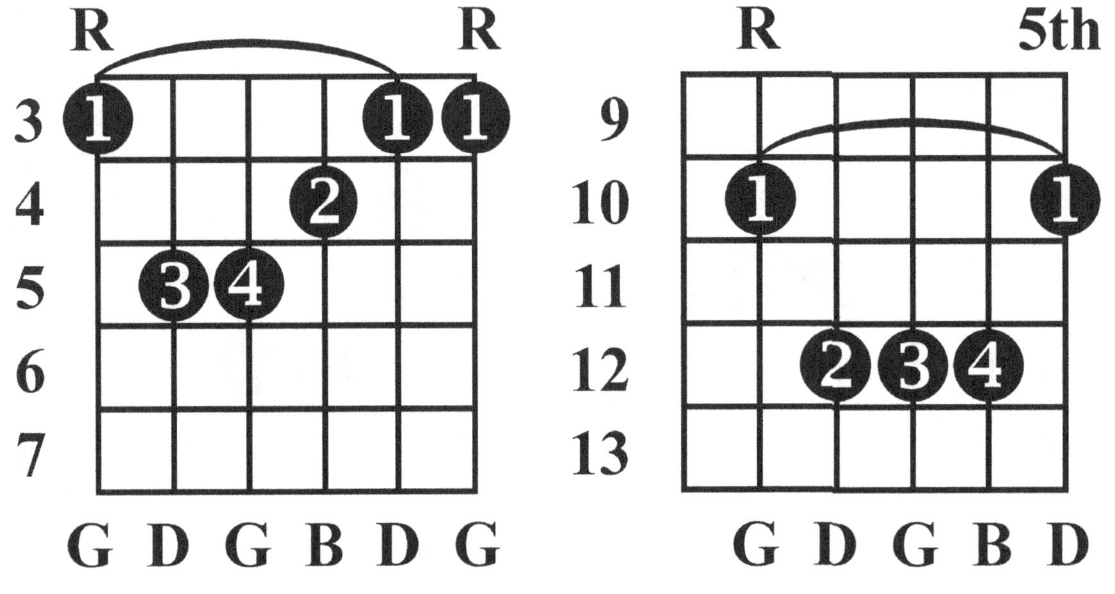

DMajor

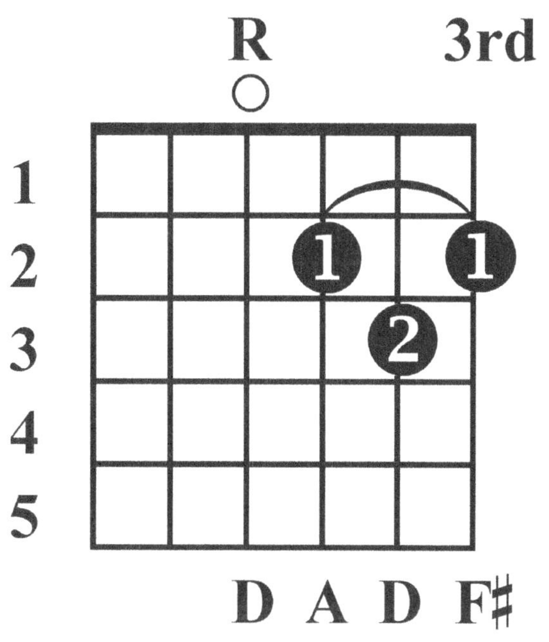

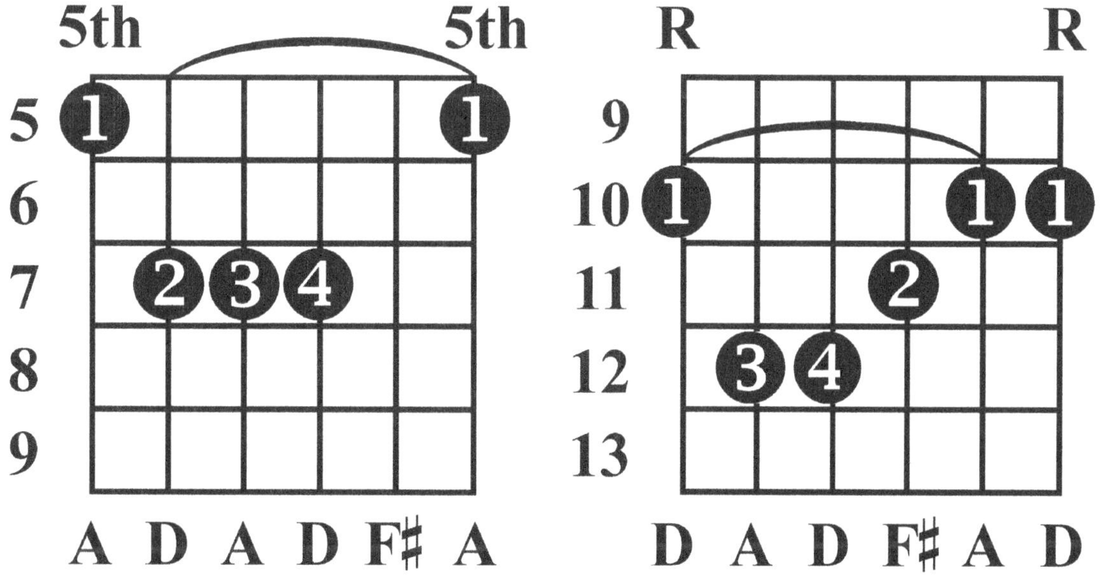

A Major

R
5th
1
2
3
4
5
A E A C♯ E

R
R
5
6
7
8
9
A E A C♯ E A

R
5th
9
10
11
12
13
A C♯ E A C♯

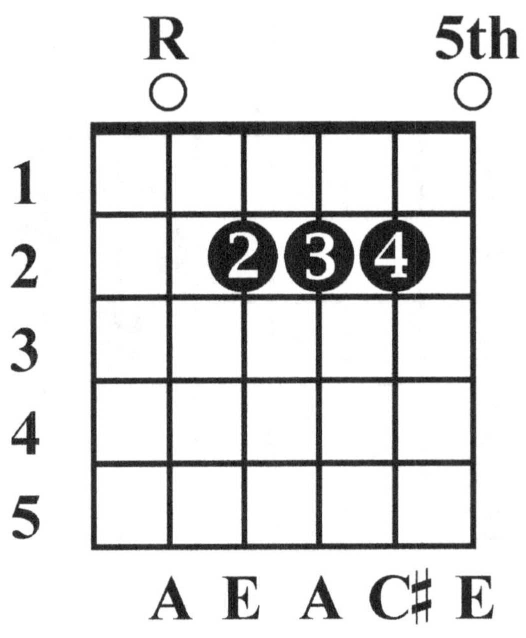

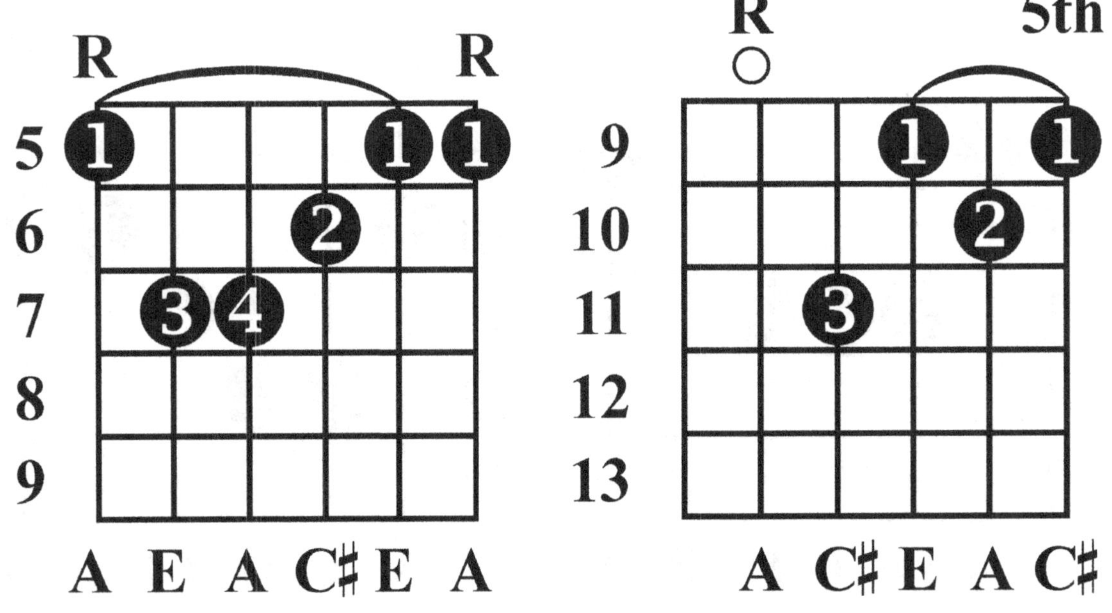

EMajor

R
R
1
2
3
E B E G♯ B E

5th
5th
B E B E G♯ B
R
R
E B E G♯ B E

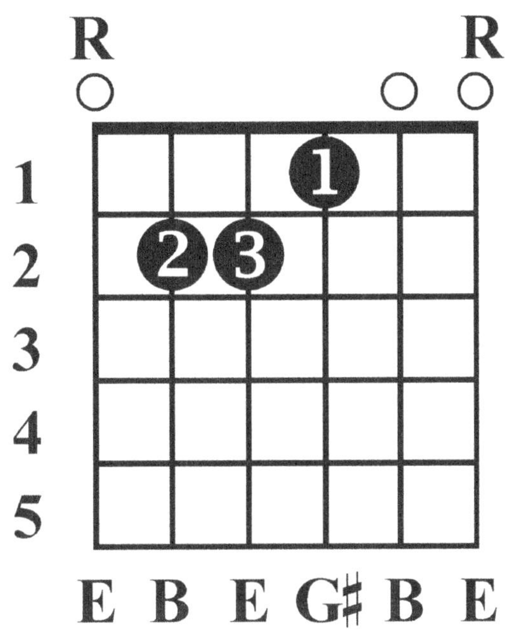

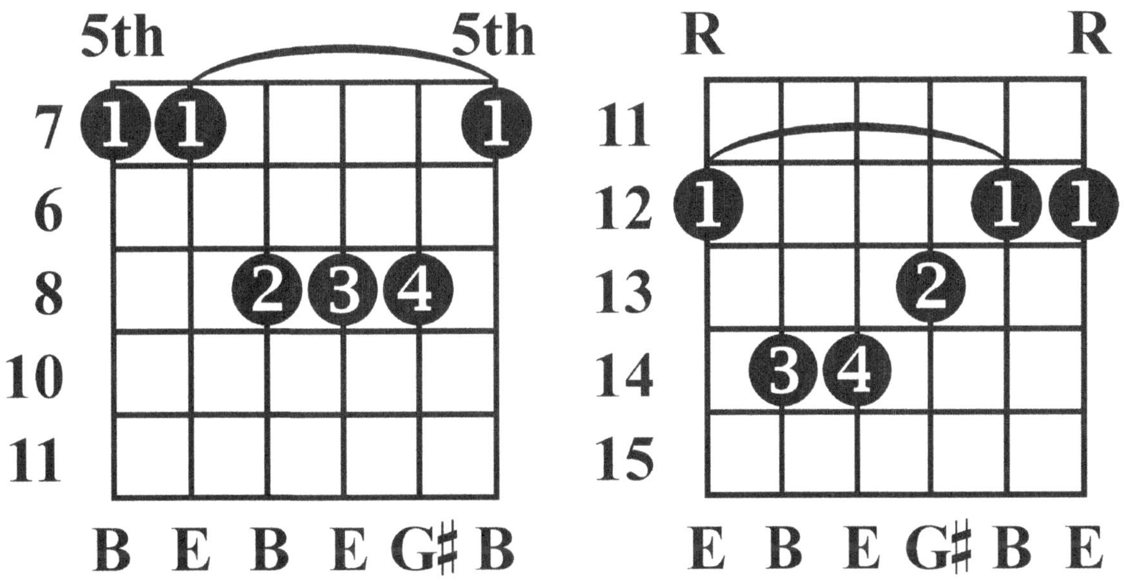

B Major

R
5th
1
2
3
4
5
1
1
2 3 4
B F# B D# F#

R
R
7
6
8
10
11
1
1 1
2
3 4
B F# B D# F# B
3rd
3rd
11
12
13
14
15
1 1
2
3
D# F# B D#

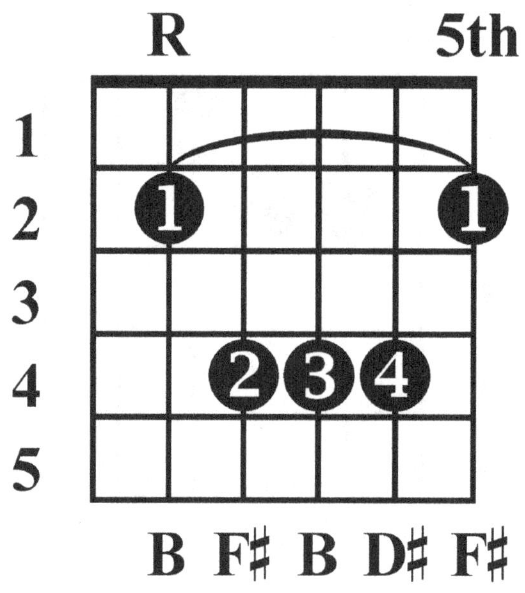

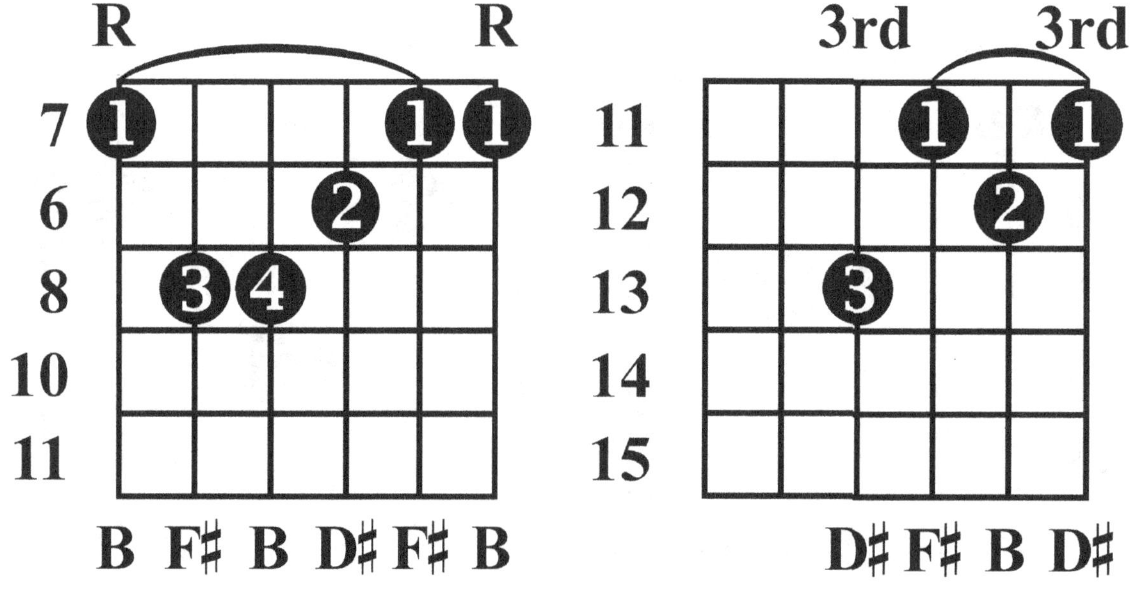

FMajor

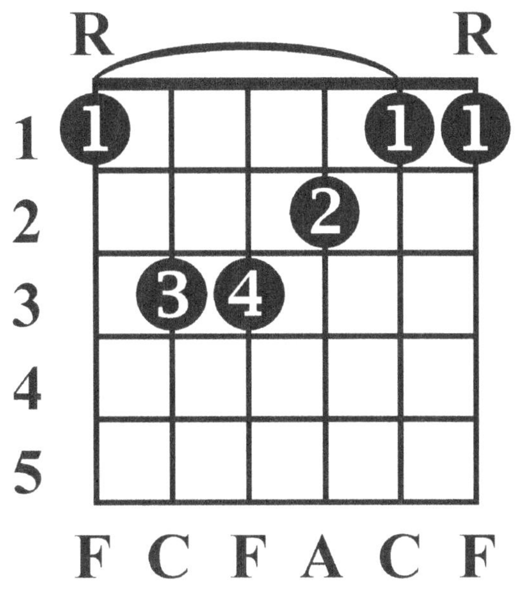

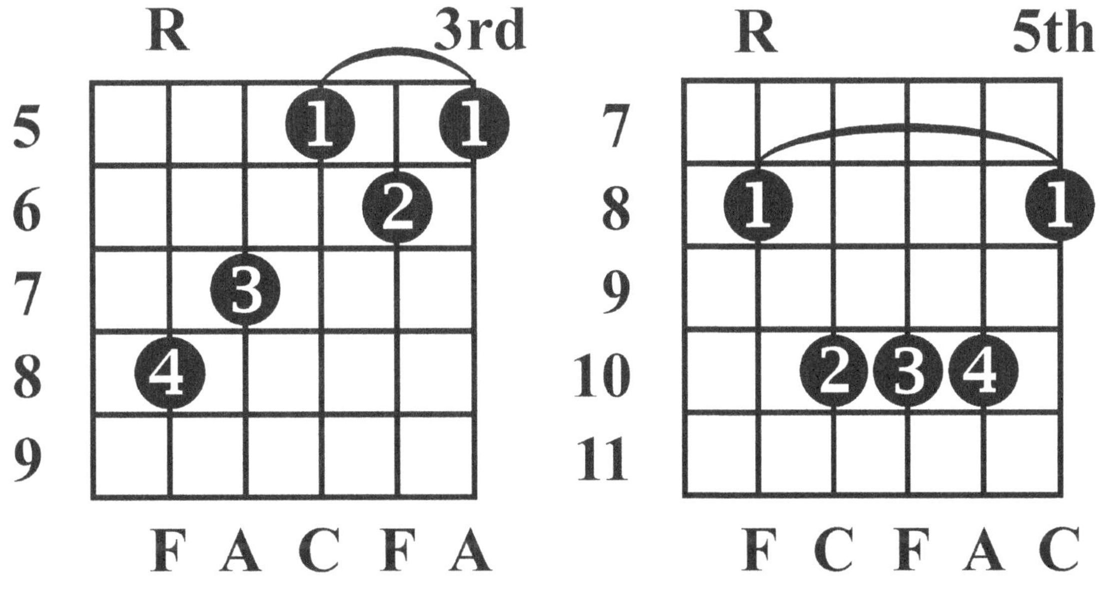

B♭ Major

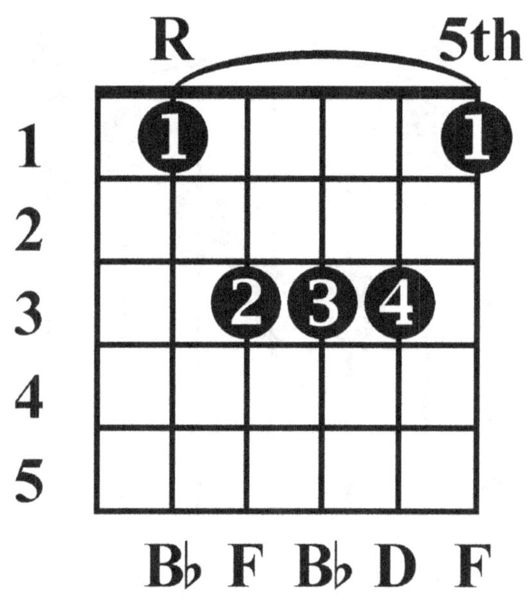

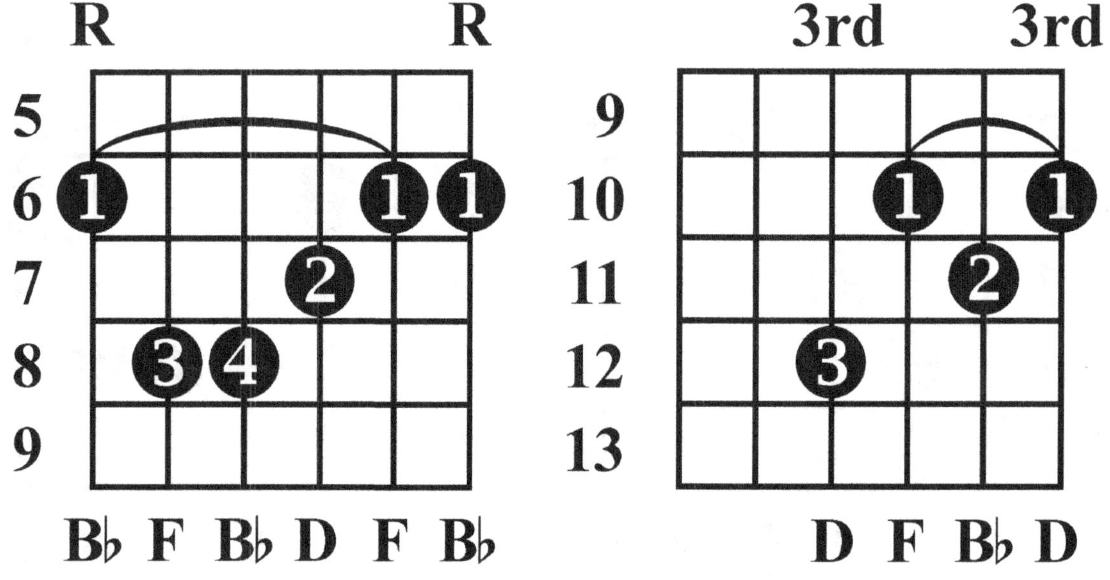

E♭ Major

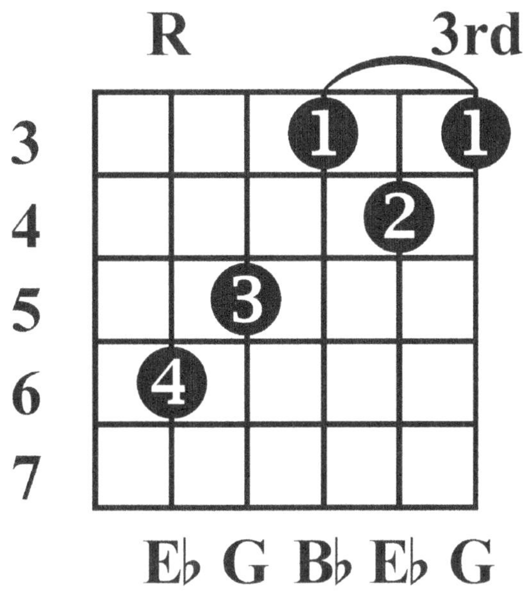

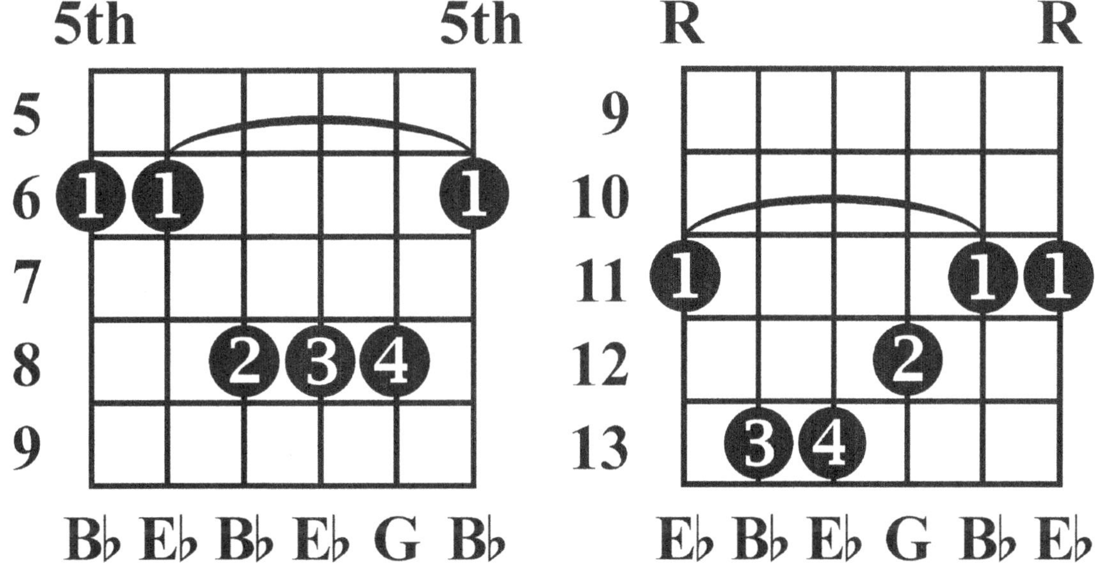

A♭ Major

5th   R
1
2
3
4
5
E♭ A♭ C A♭

R   R
3
4
5
6
7
A♭ E♭ A♭ C E♭ A♭

R   5th
11
12
13
14
15
A♭ E♭ A♭ C E♭

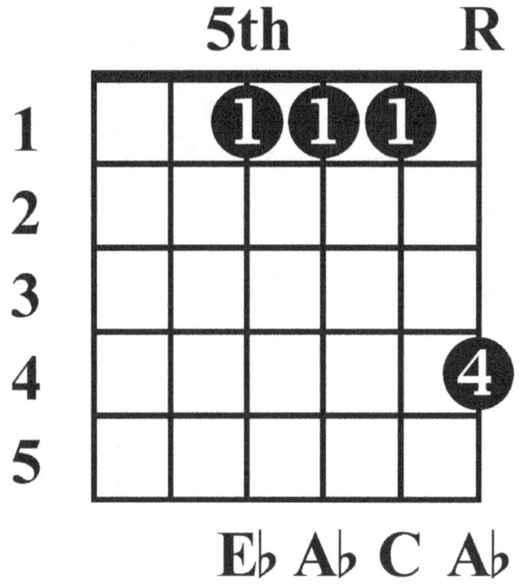

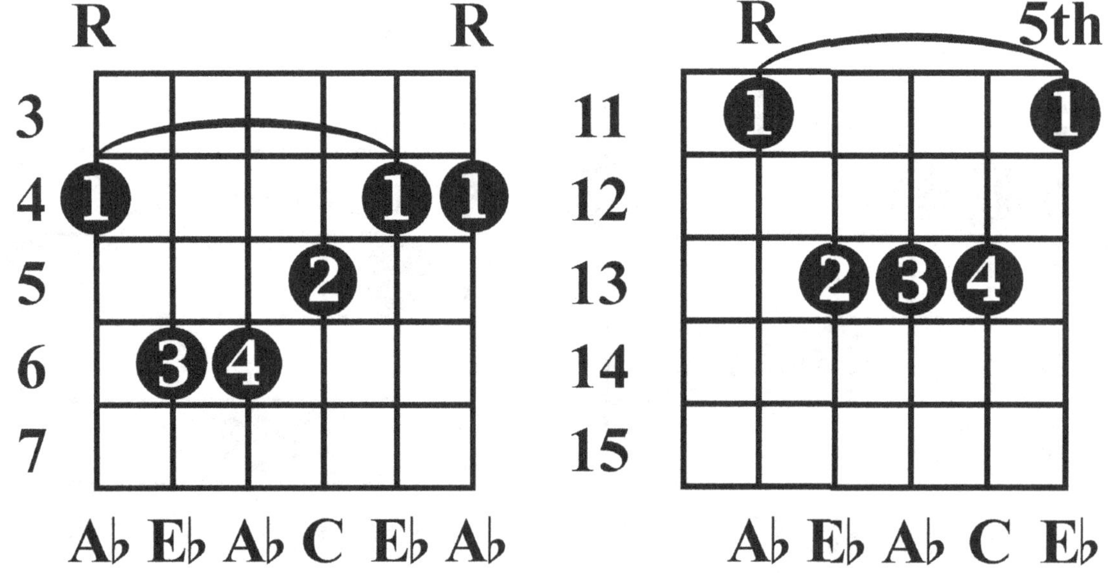

D♭ Major

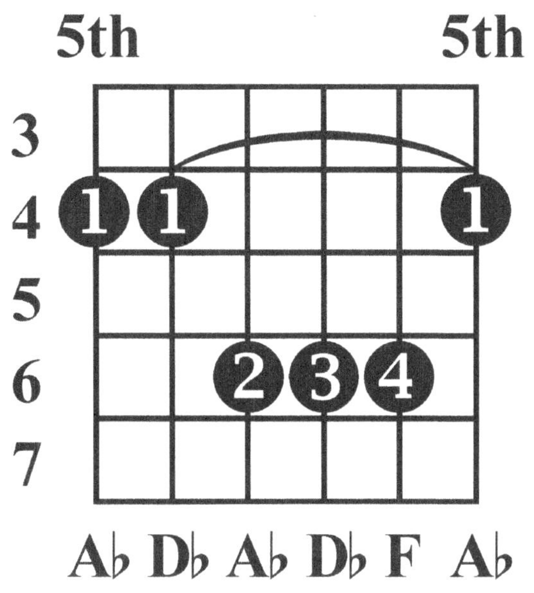

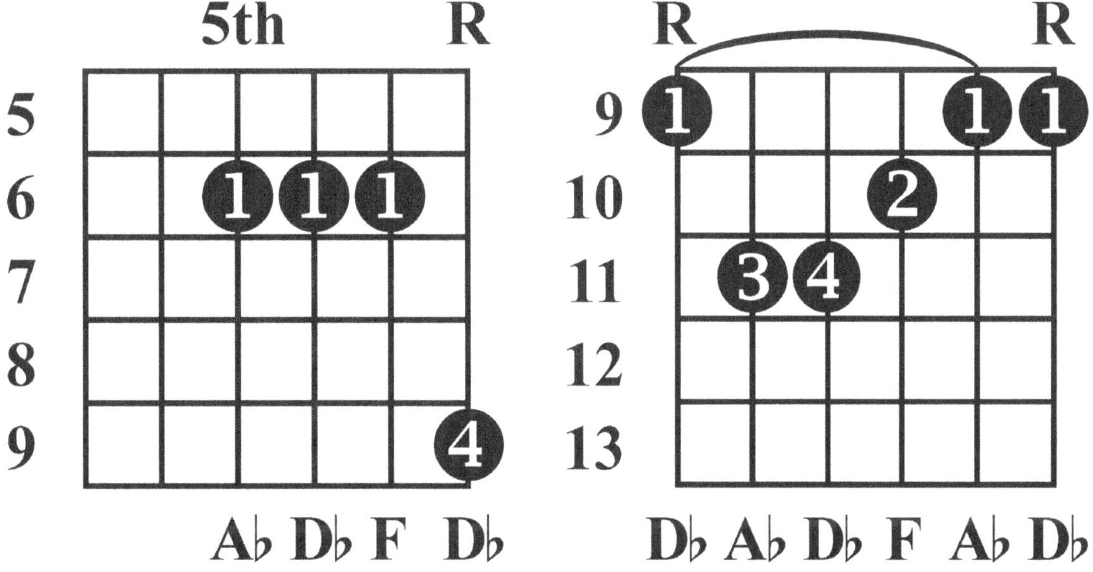

G♭ / F♯ Major

R   R
1
2
3
4
5
G♭ D♭ G♭ B♭ D♭ G♭

R   3rd
5
6
7
8
9
G♭ B♭ D♭ G♭ B♭
R   5th
9
10
11
12
13
G♭ D♭ G♭ B♭ D♭

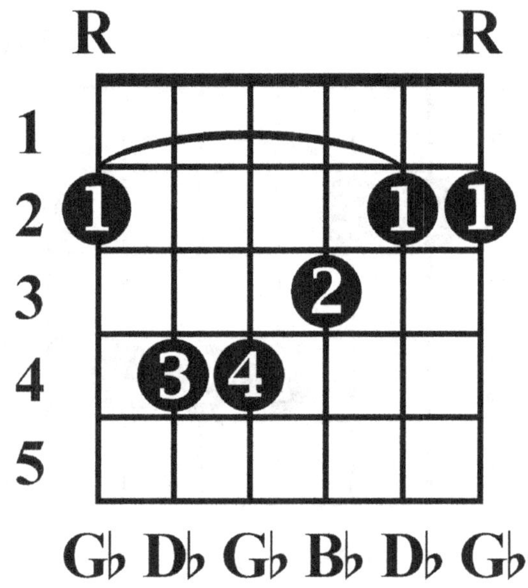

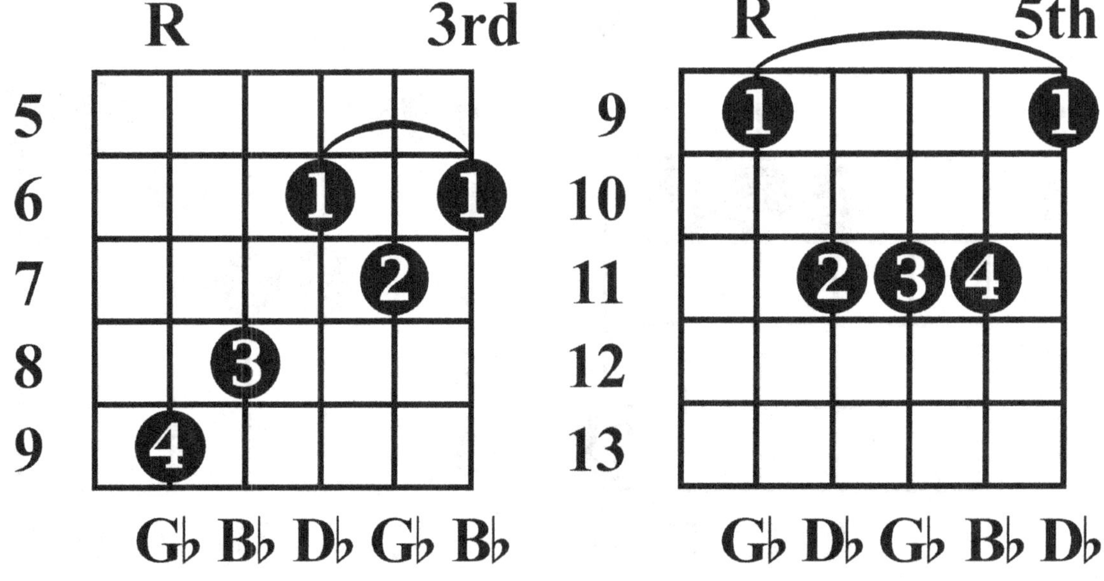

CMinor

♭3rd   5th
1
2
3
4
5
E♭ G C G

R   5th
3
4
5
6
7
C G C E♭ C

R   R
7
8
9
10
11
C G C E♭ G C

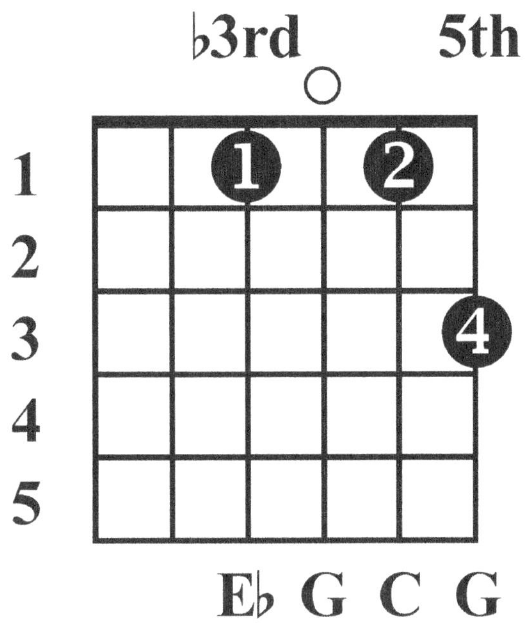

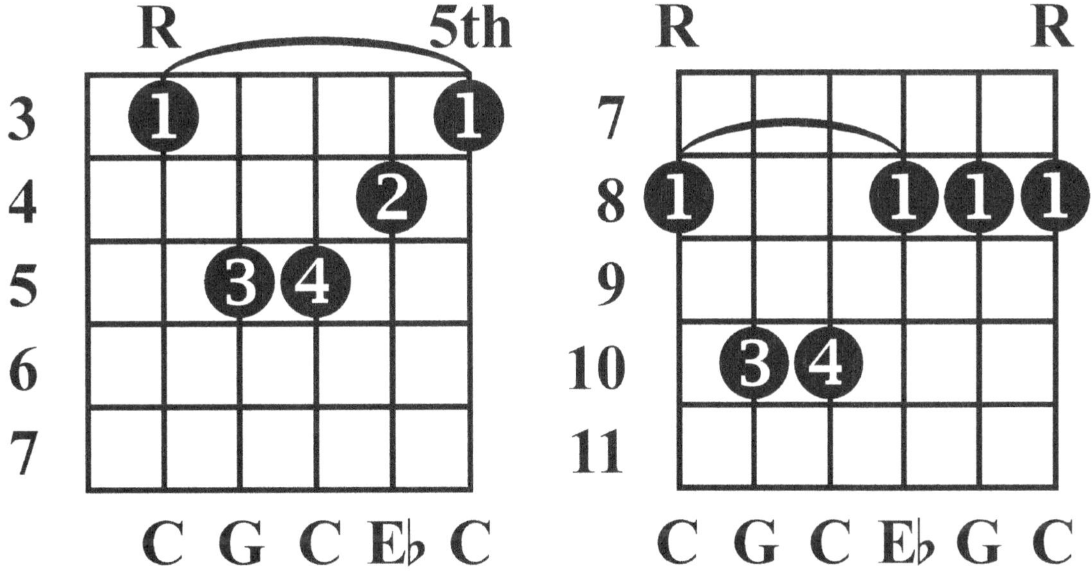

GMinor

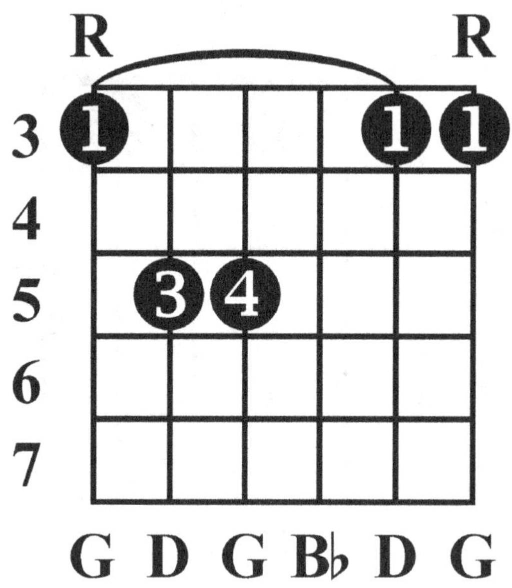

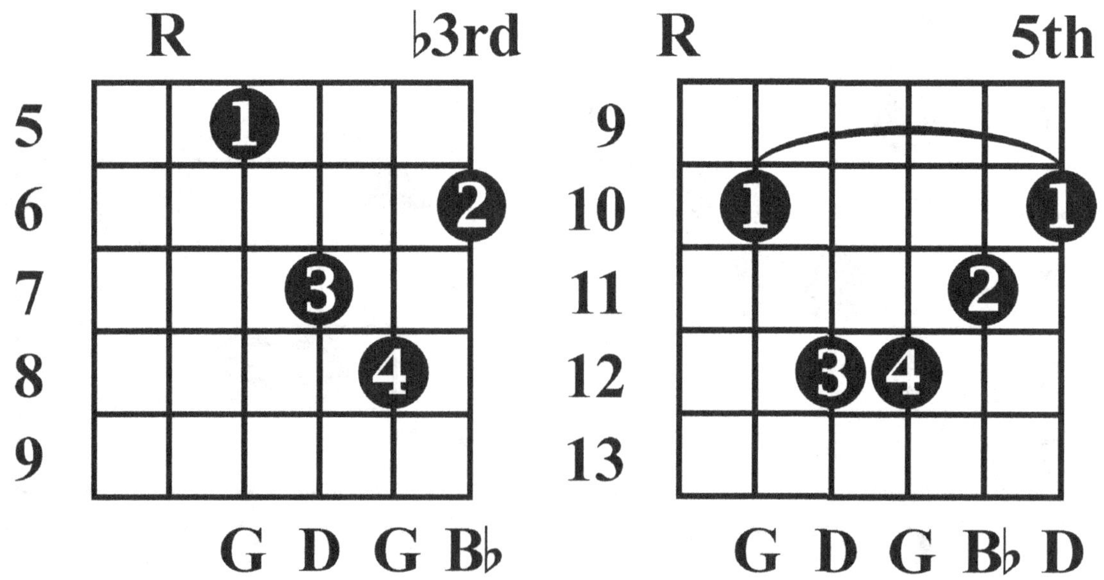

DMinor

R   ♭3rd
1
2
3
4
5
D A D F

R   5th
5
6
7
8
9
D A D F A

R   R
9
10
11
12
13
D A D F A D

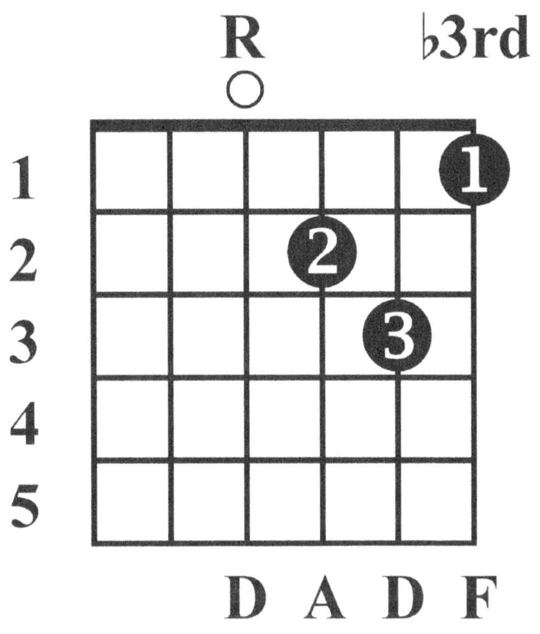

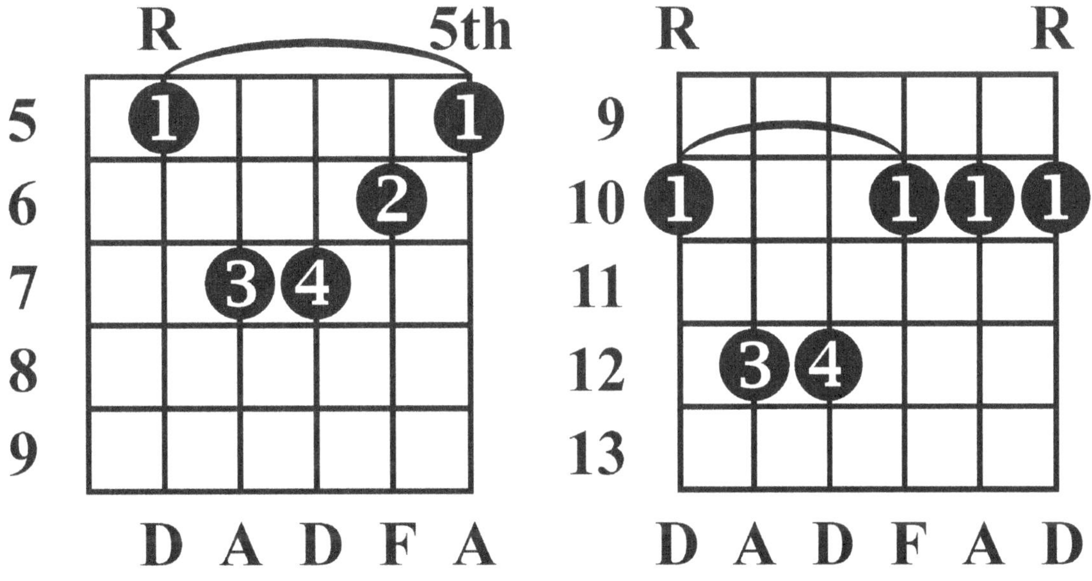

A Minor

R
5th
1
2
3
4
5
A E A C E

R
R
5
6
7
8
9
A E A C E A
R
b3rd
7
8
9
10
11
A E A C

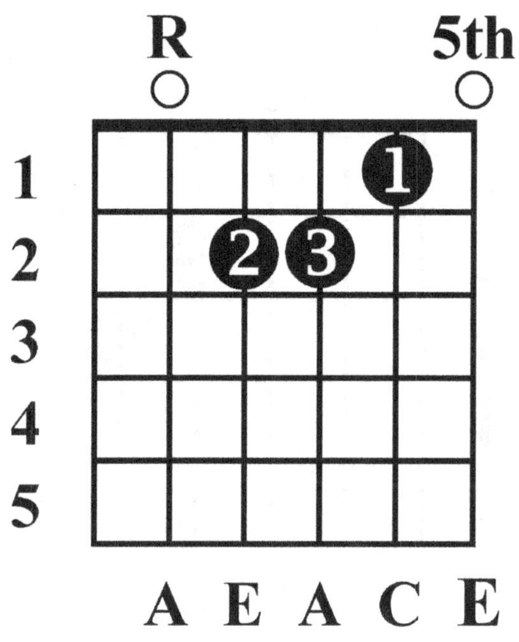

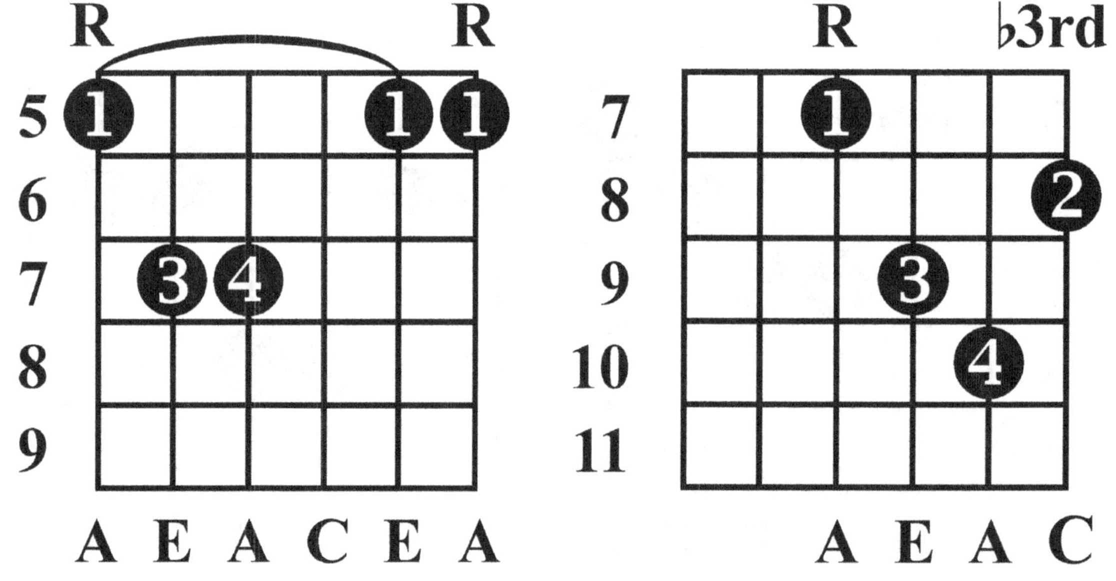

EMinor

R
R
1
2
3
4
5
2 3
E B E G B E

R
♭3rd
1
2
3
4
5
1
2
3
4
E B E G
R
5th
7
8
9
10
11
1
1
2
3 4
E B E G B

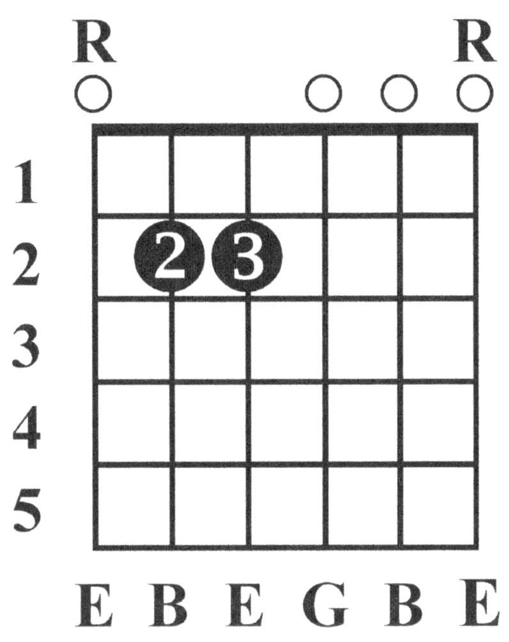

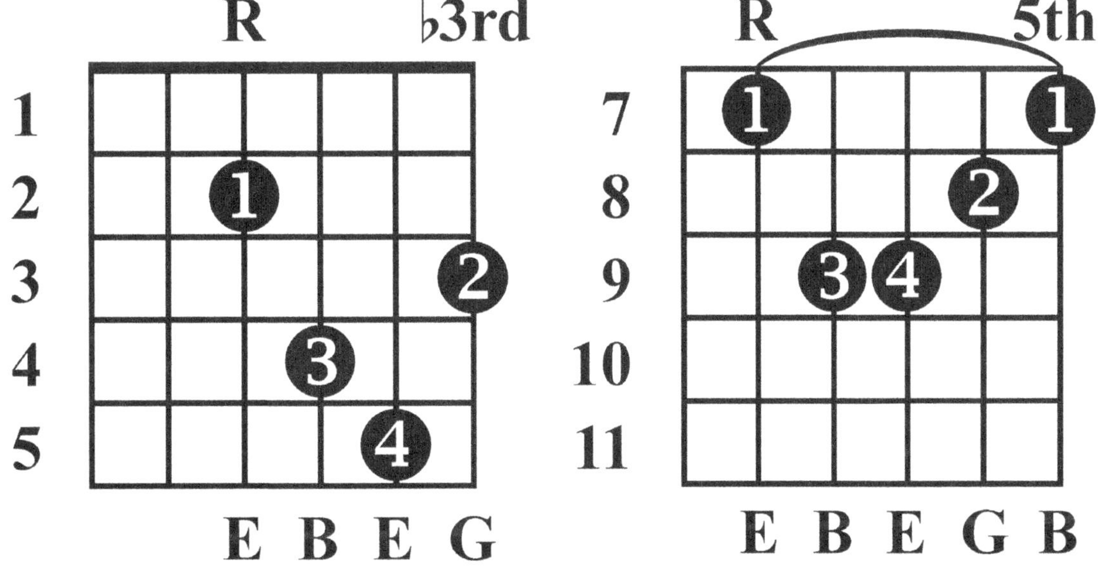

BMinor

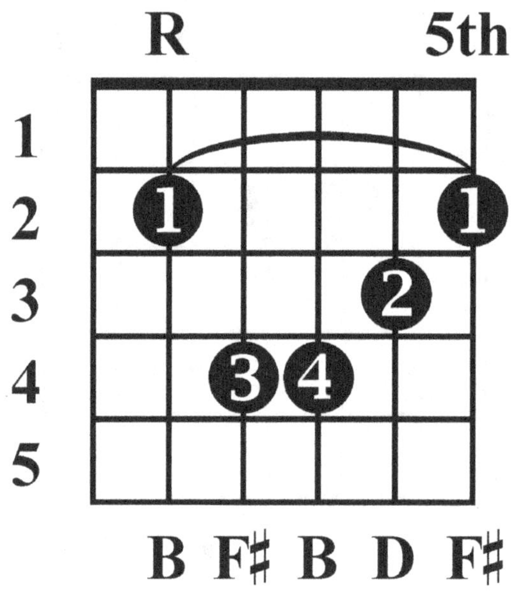

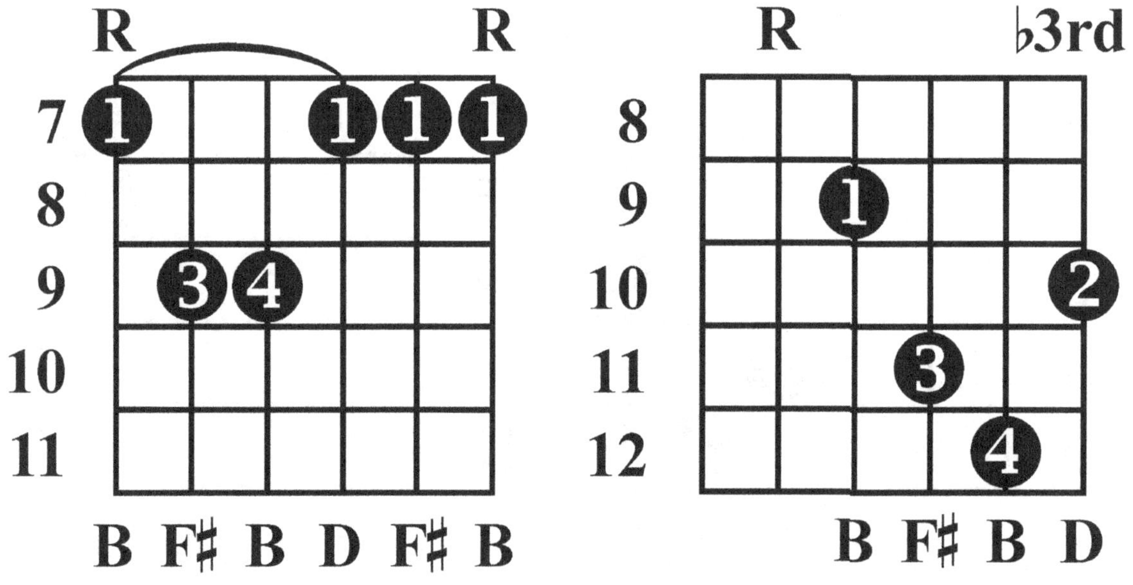

FMinor

R   R
1 1 1
3 4
F C F A♭ C F

R   ♭3rd
1
2
3
4
F C F A♭

R   5th
1   1
2
3 4
F C F A♭ C

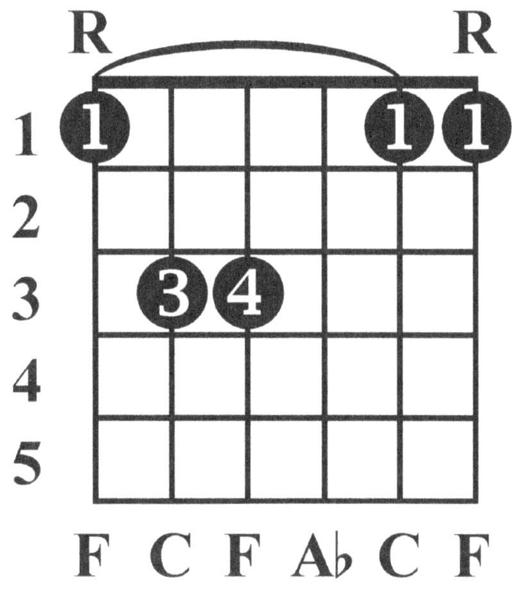

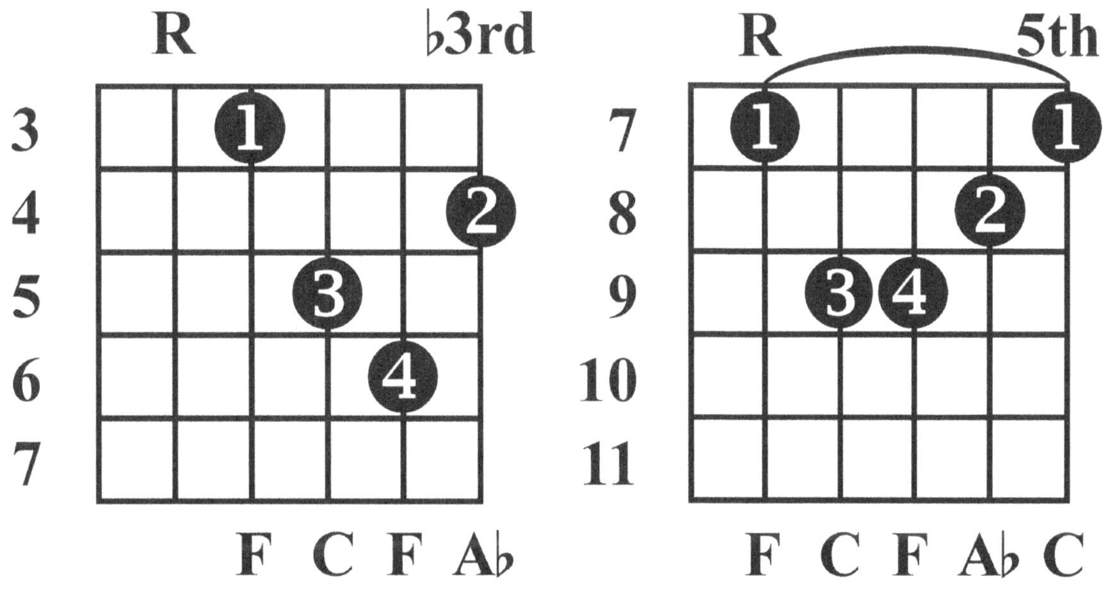

B♭ Minor

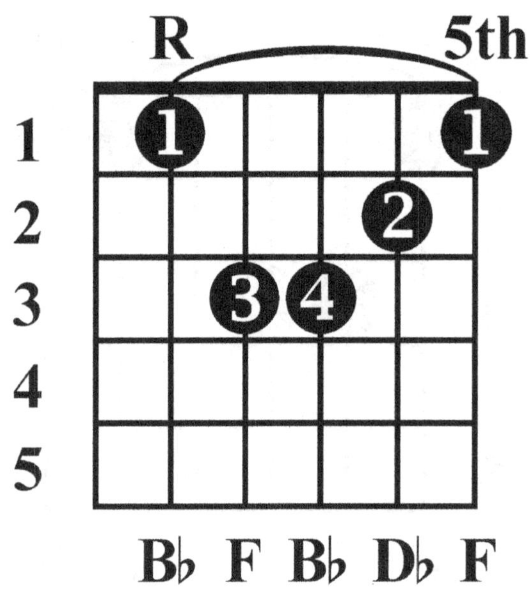

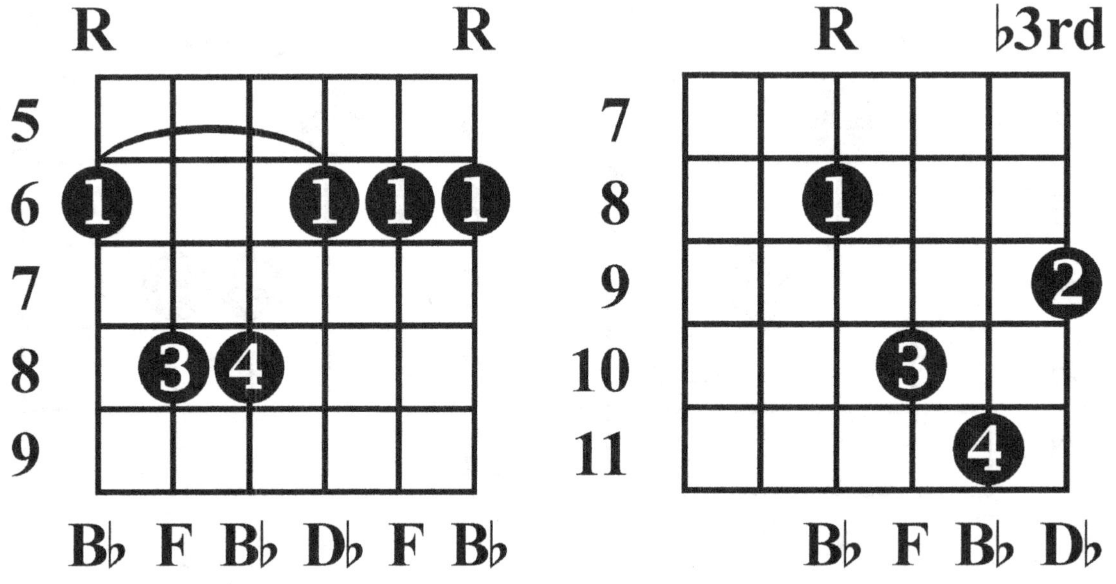

E♭ Minor

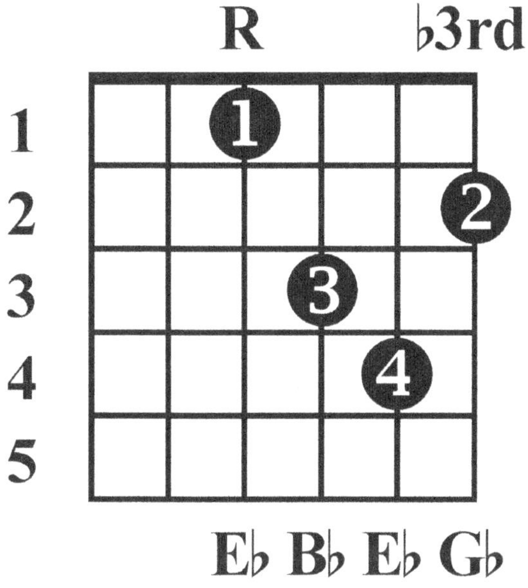

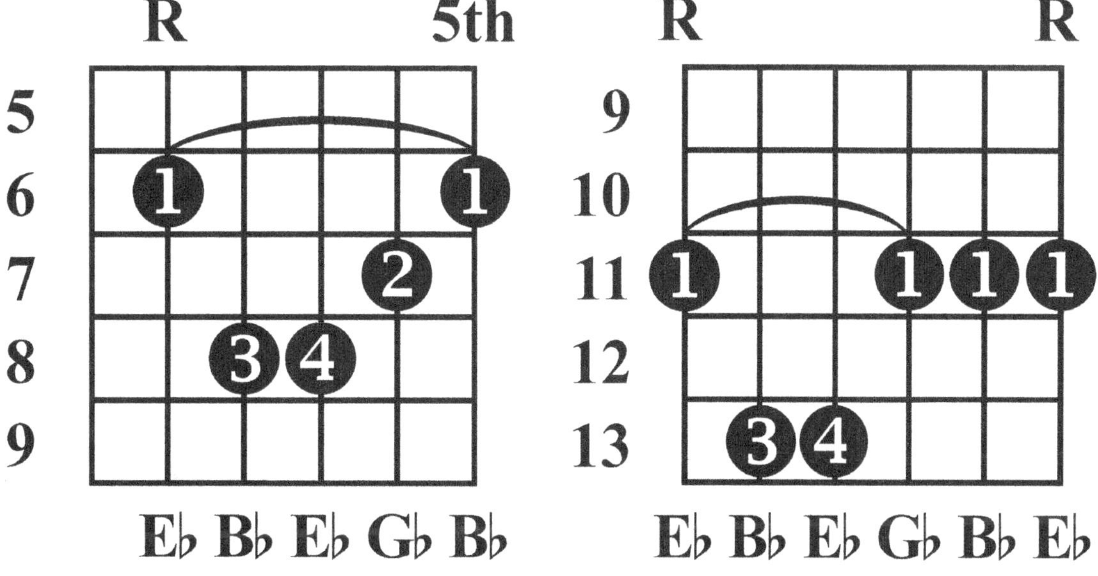

A♭Minor

R   R
3
4 1   1 1 1
5
6   3 4
7
A♭ E♭ A♭ C♭ E♭ A♭

R   ♭3rd
5
6   1
7   2
8   3
9   4
A♭ E♭ A♭ C♭

R   5th
9
10
11 1   1
12   2
13   3 4
A♭ E♭ A♭ C♭ E♭

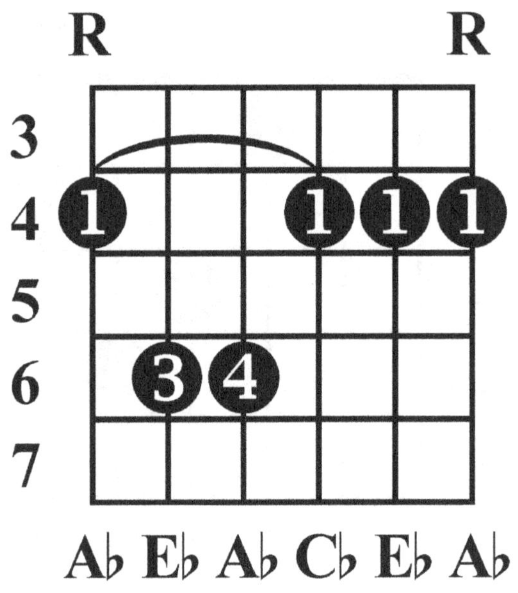

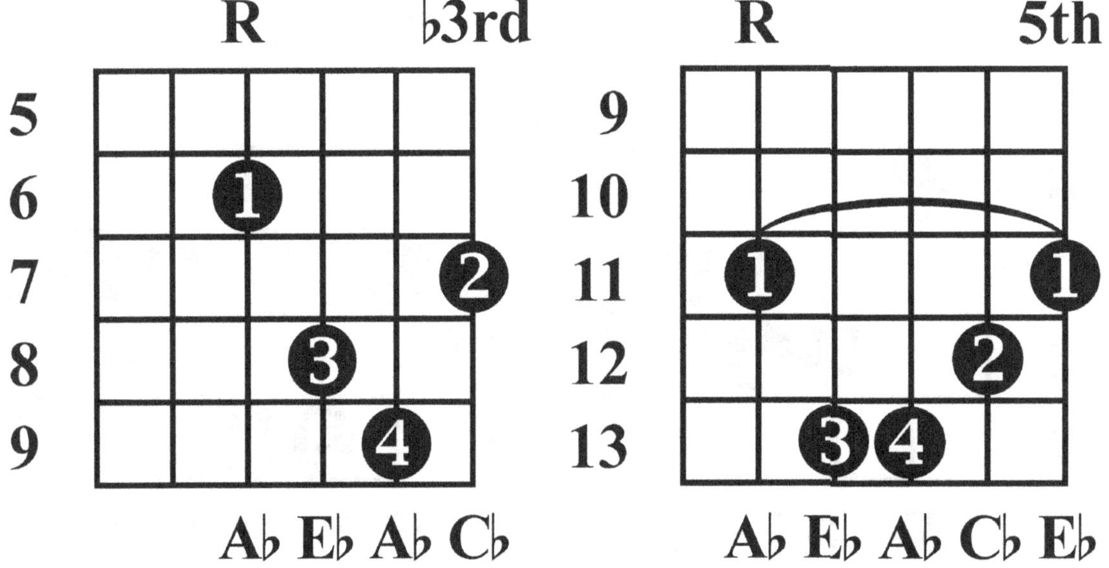

D♭Minor

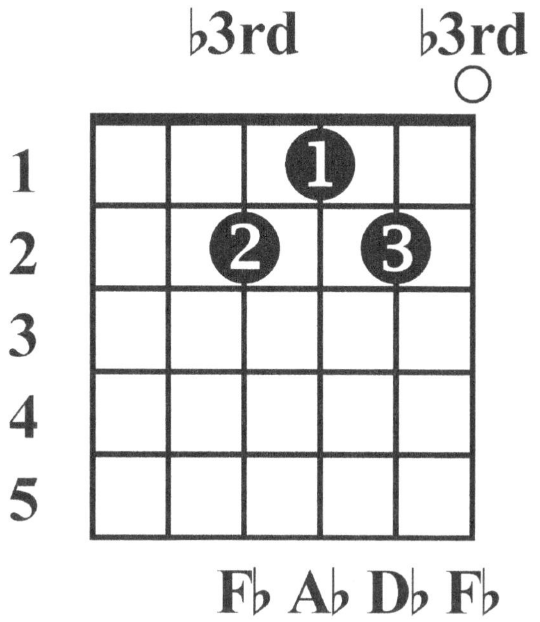

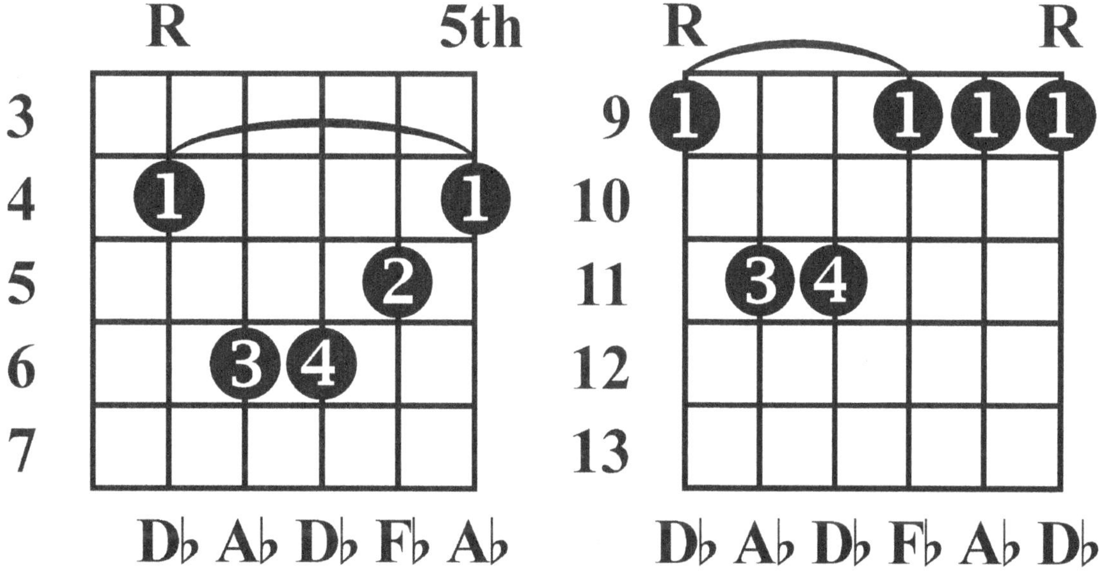

G♭ / F♯ Minor

R   R
1
2
3
4
5
G♭ D♭ G♭ B♭♭ D♭ G♭

R   ♭3rd
3
4
5
6
7
G♭ D♭ G♭ B♭♭
R   5th
9
10
11
12
13
G♭ D♭ G♭ B♭♭ D♭

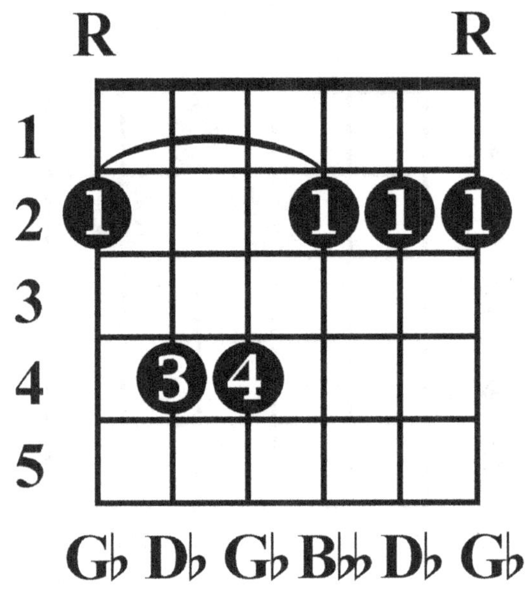

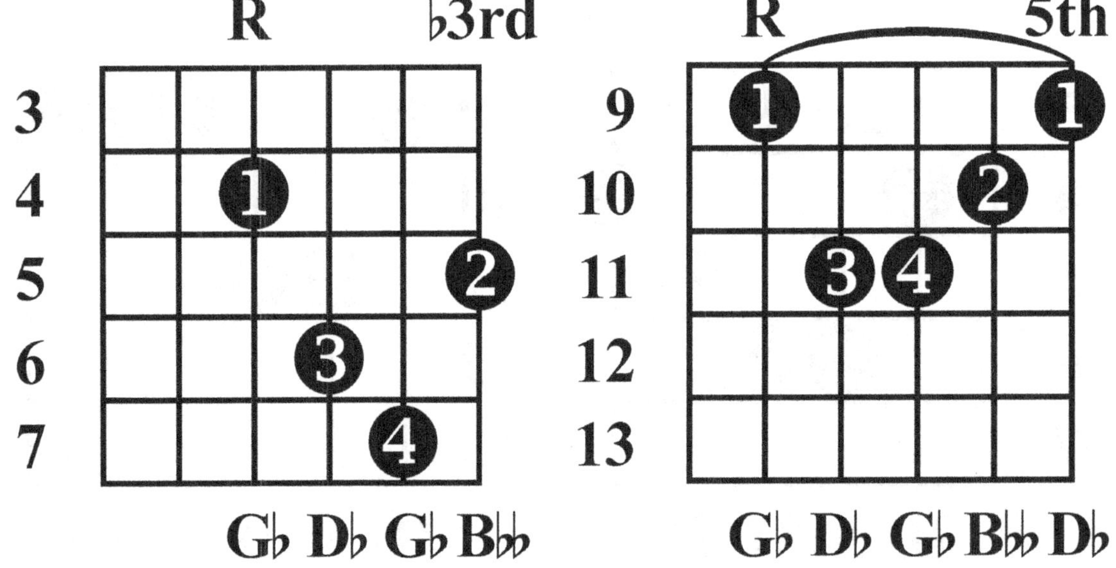

C7

R
3rd
1
2
3
4
5
C E B♭ C E

R
5th
3
4
5
6
7
C G B♭ E G
R
R
7
8
9
10
11
C G B♭ E G C

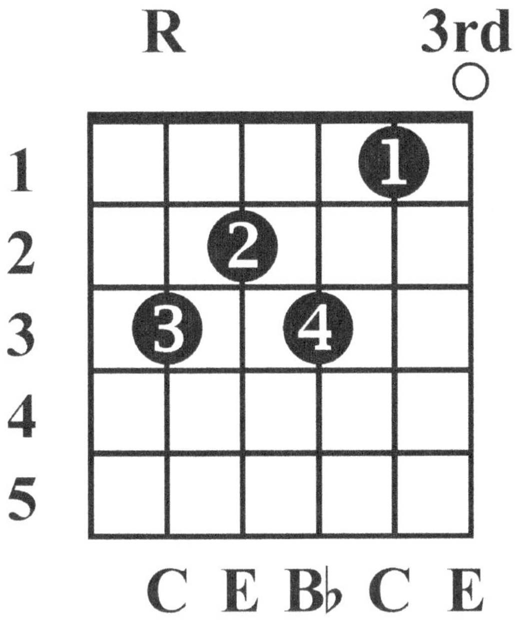

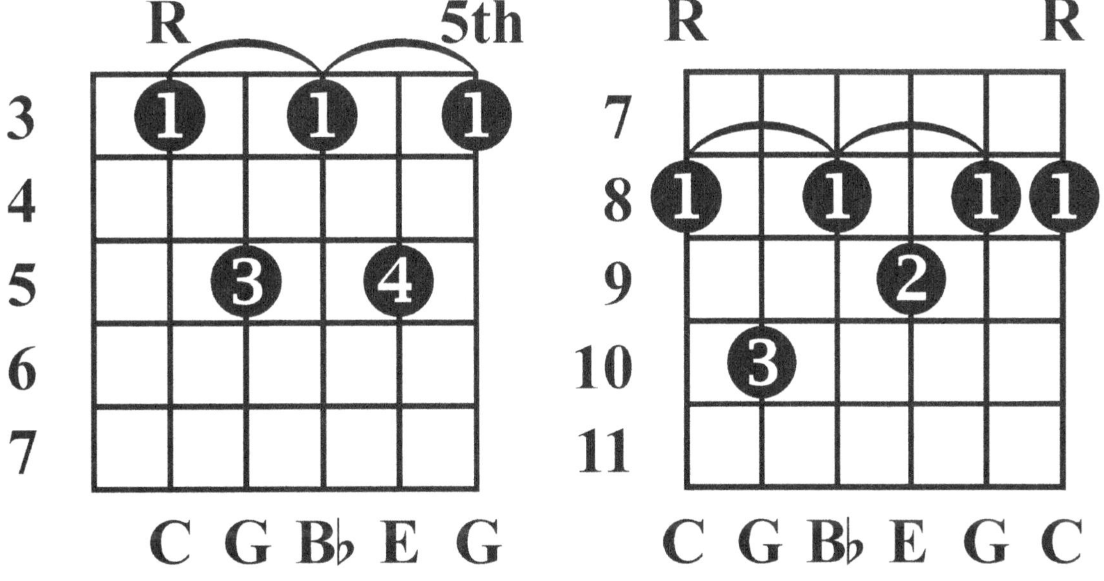

G7

R 7th
1
2
3
4
5
G B D G B F

R R
3
4
5
6
7
G D F B D G

R 5th
9
10
11
12
13
G D F B G

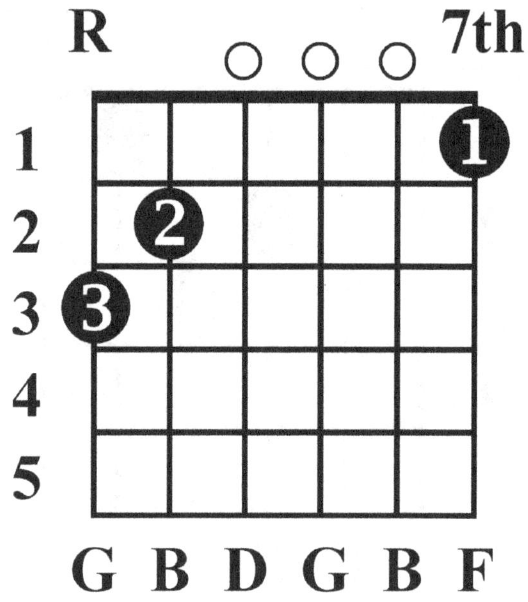

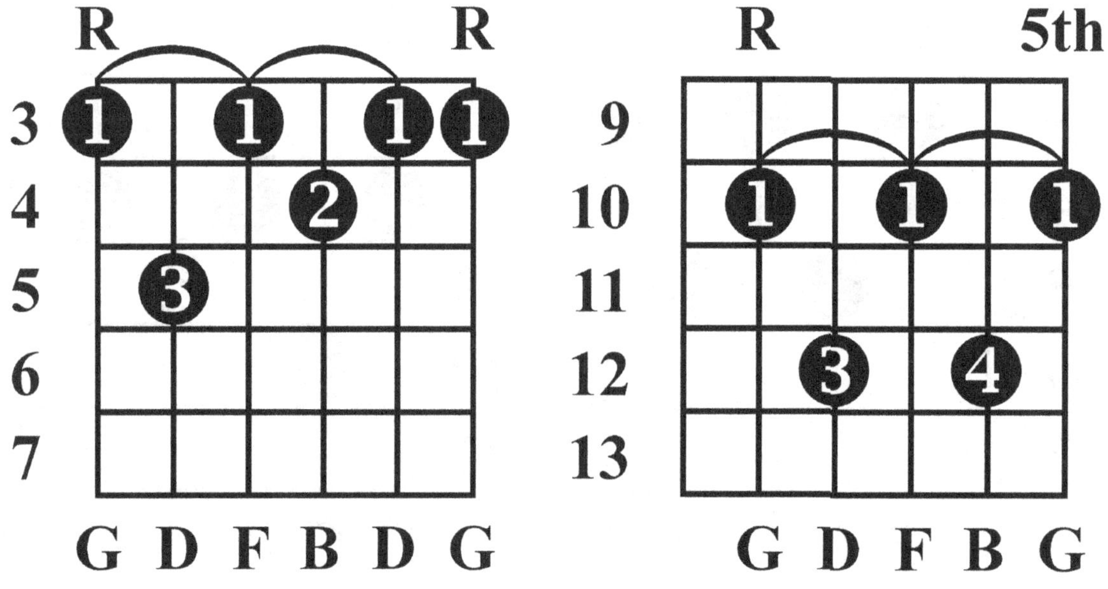

D7

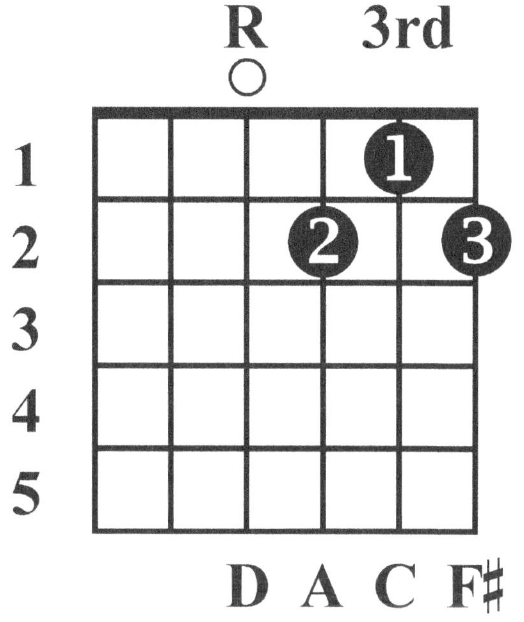

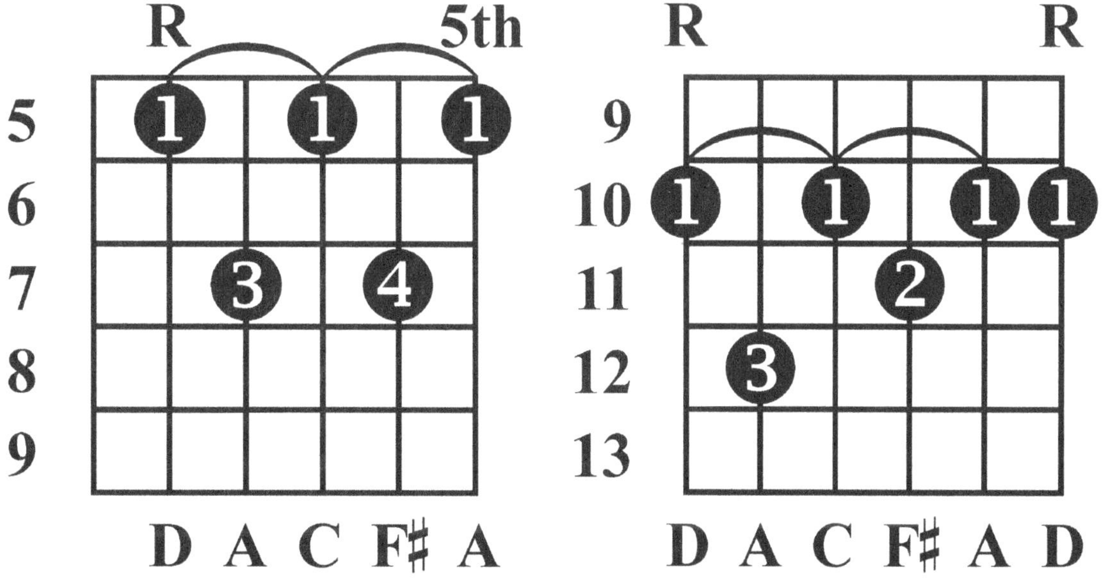

A7

R
5th
1
2
3
4
5
A E G C♯ E

R
7th
1
2
3
4
5
A E A C♯ G
R
R
5
6
7
8
9
A E G C♯ E A

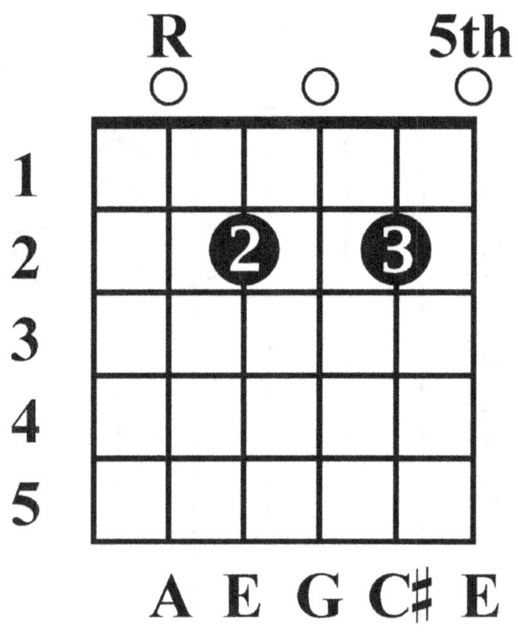

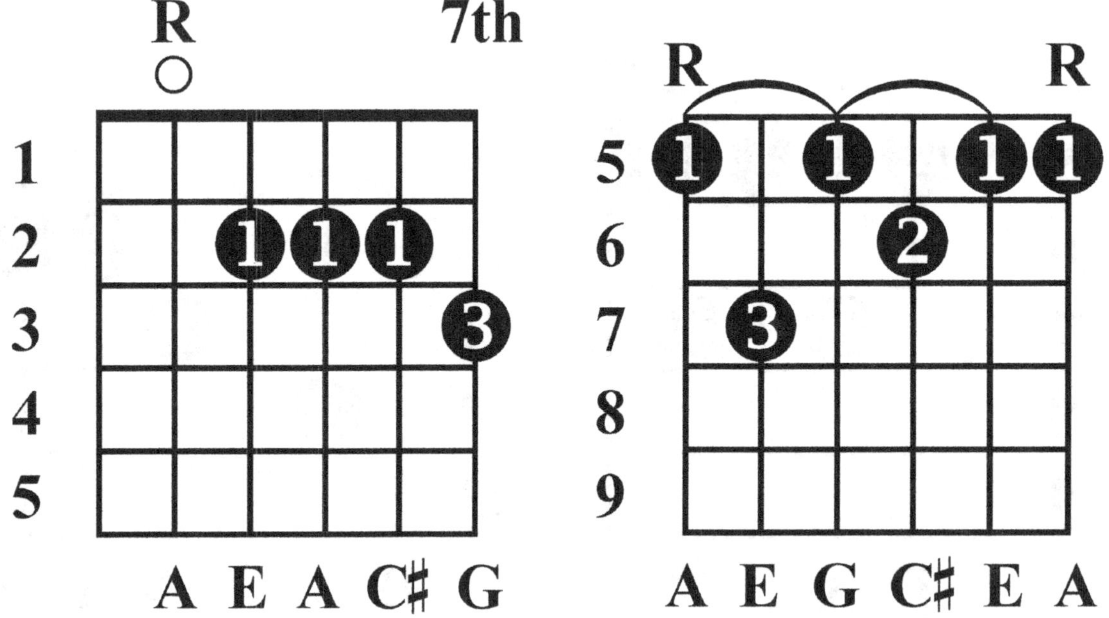

E7

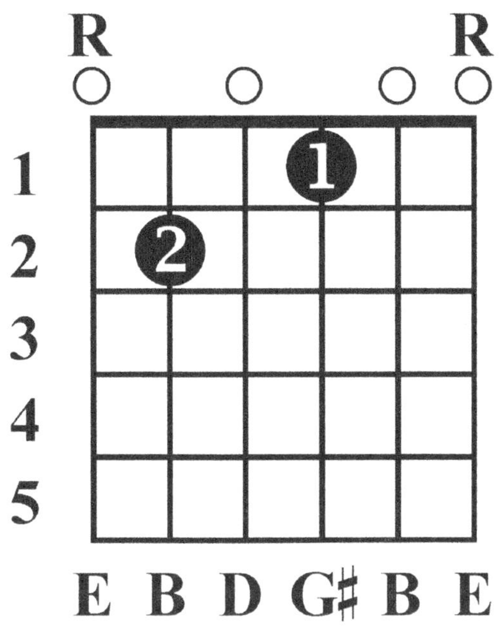

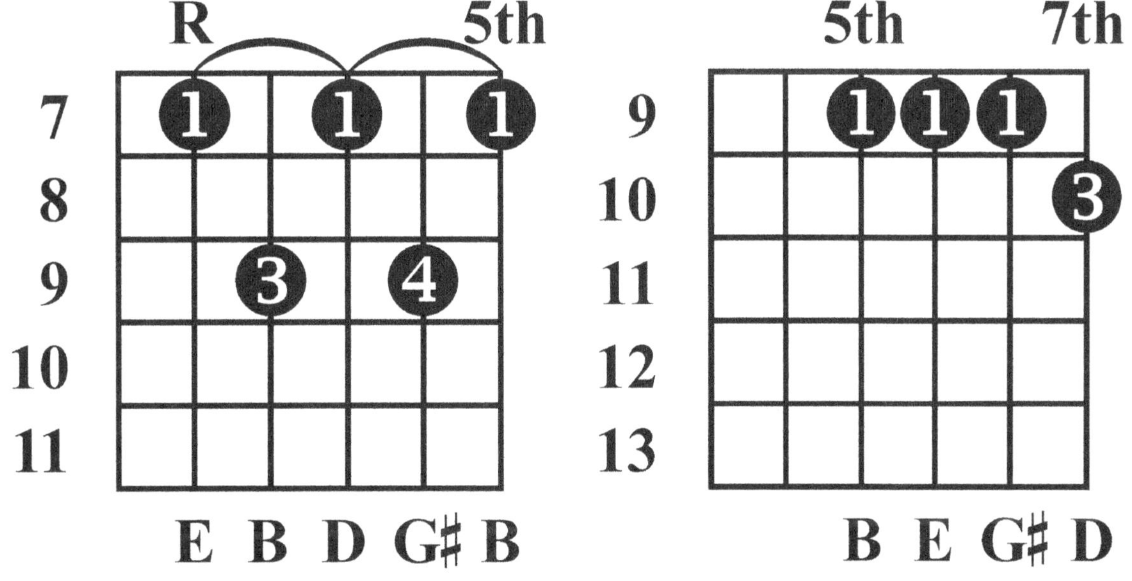

B7

R
5th
1
2
3
4
5
B D# A B F#

R
5th
1
2
3
4
5
B F# A D# F#
R
R
7
8
9
10
11
B F# A D# F# B

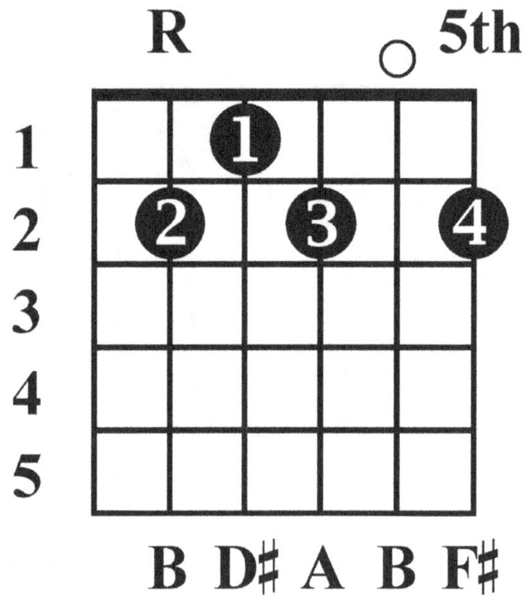

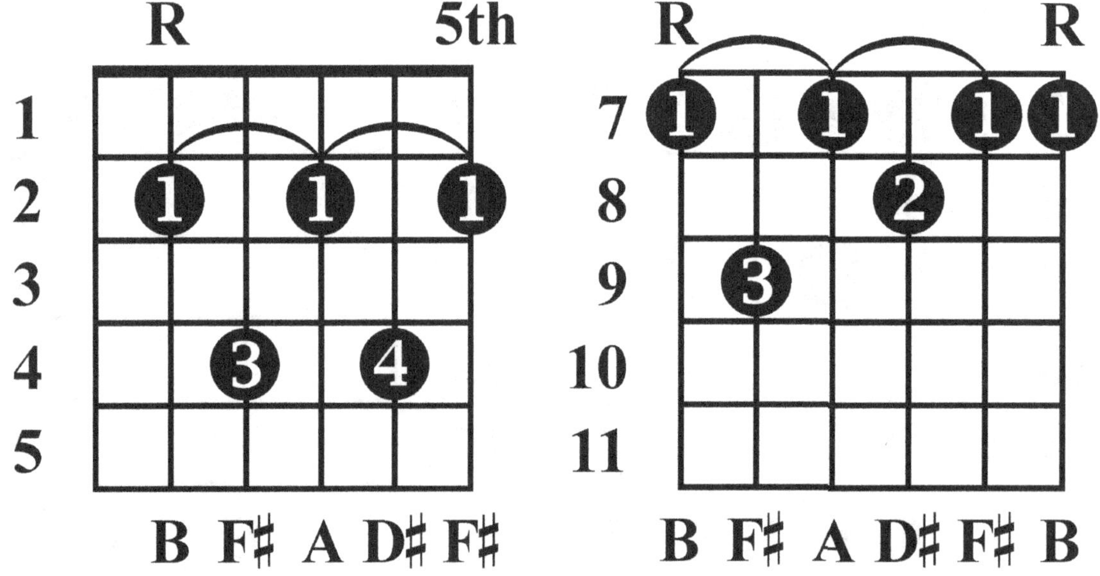

F7

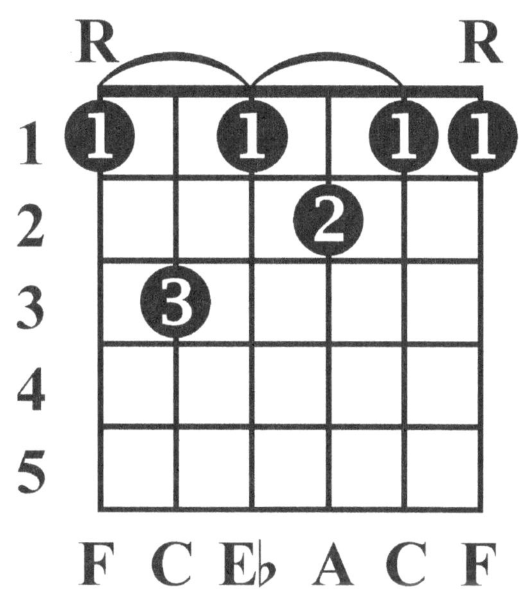

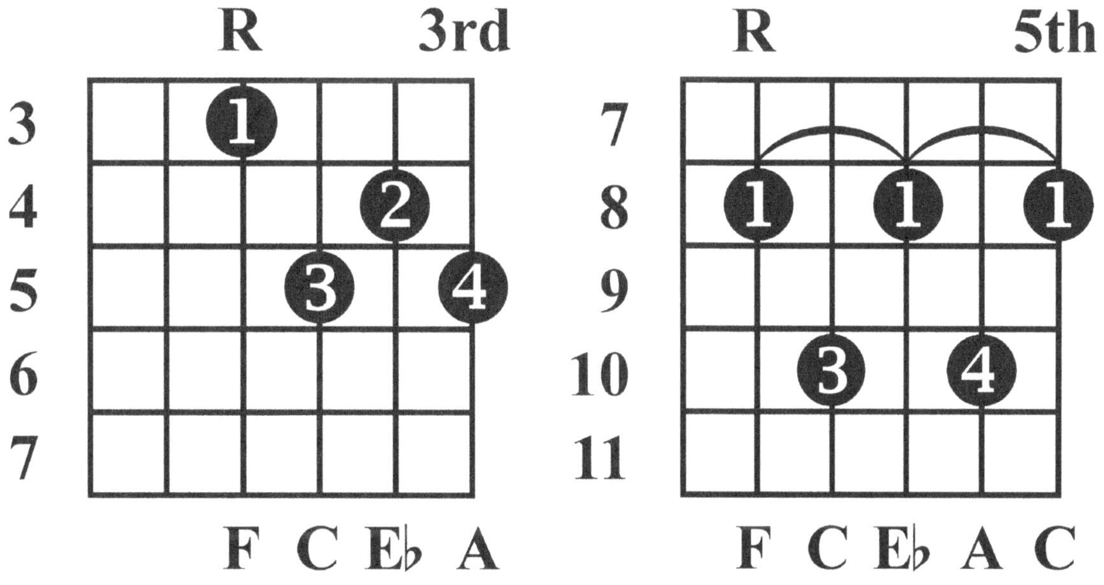

B♭7

R
5th
1
2
3
4
5
1
1
1
3
4
B♭ F A♭ D F

5th
7th
3
4
5
6
7
1
1
1
3
F B♭ D A♭
R
R
5
6
7
8
9
1
1
1
1
2
3
B♭ F A♭ D F B♭

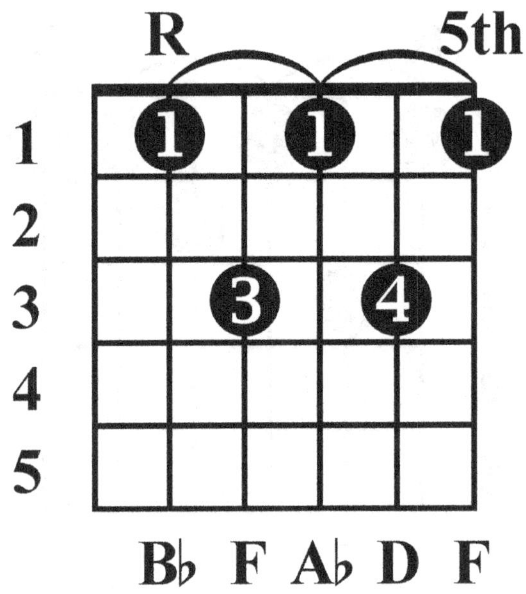

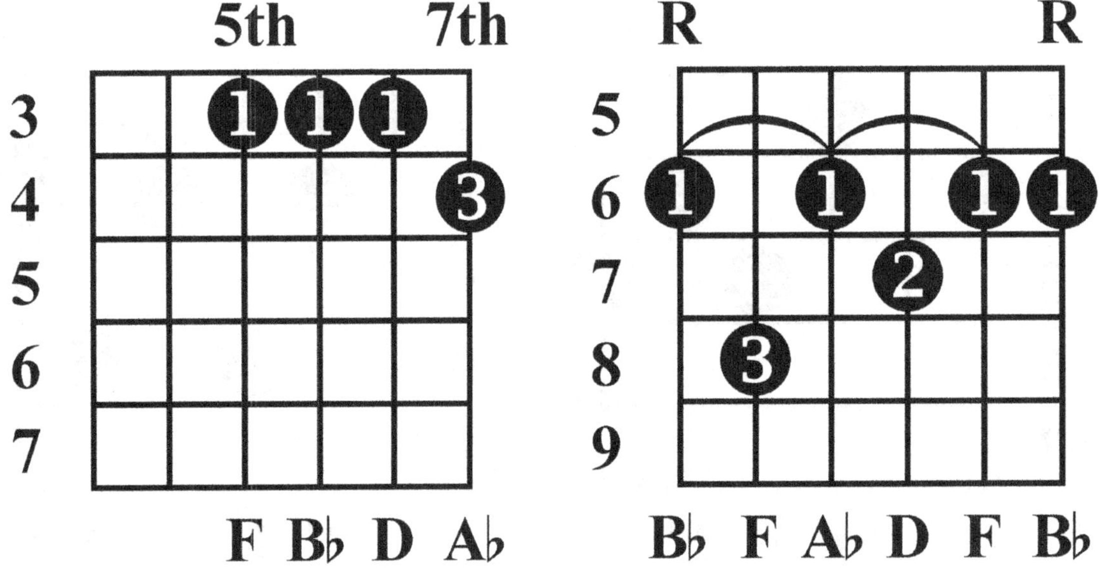

E♭7

R
3rd
1
2
3
4
5
E♭ B♭ D♭ G

R
5th
6
7
8
9
10
E♭ B♭ D♭ G B♭
R
R
10
11
12
13
14
E♭ B♭ D♭ G B♭ E♭

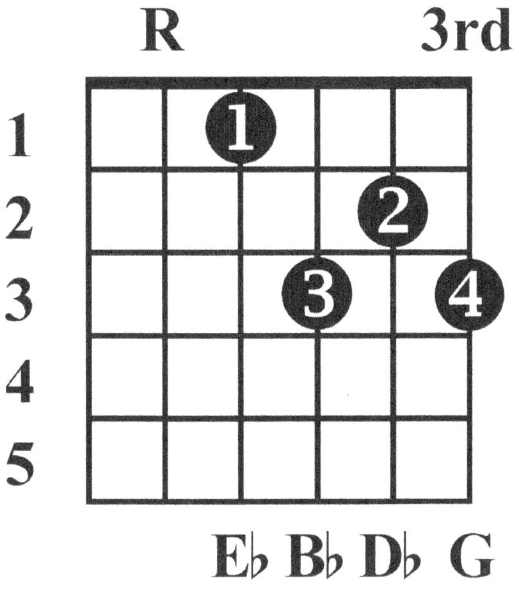

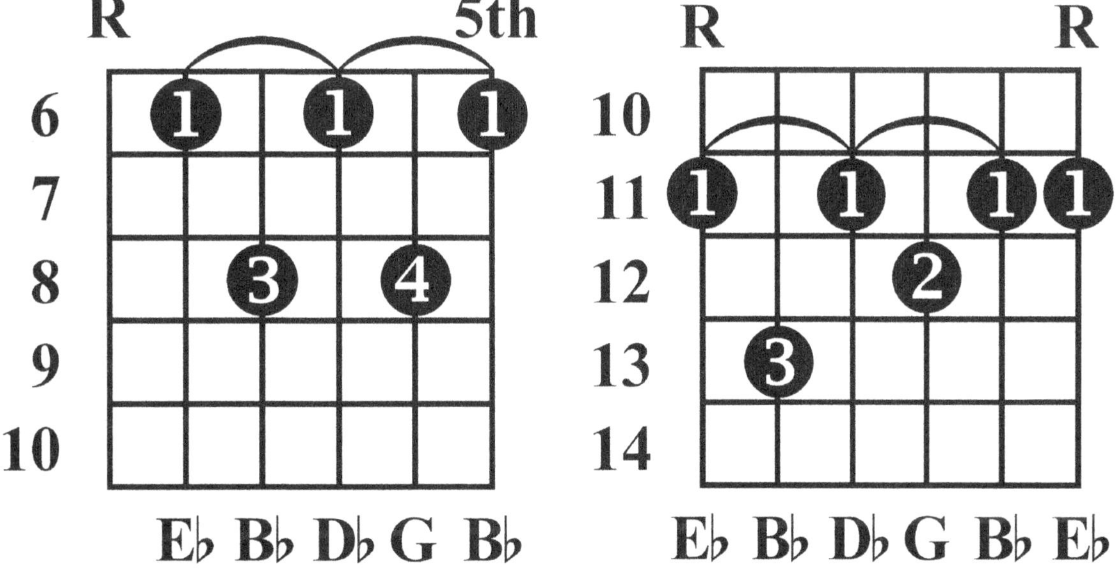

A♭7

5th
7th
1
2
3
4
5
E♭ A♭ C G♭

R
R
3
4
5
6
7
A♭ E♭ G♭ C E♭ A♭
R
5th
11
12
13
14
15
A♭ E♭ G♭ C E♭

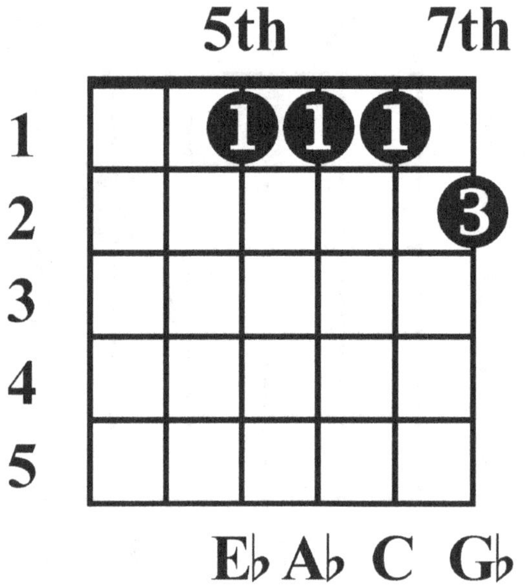

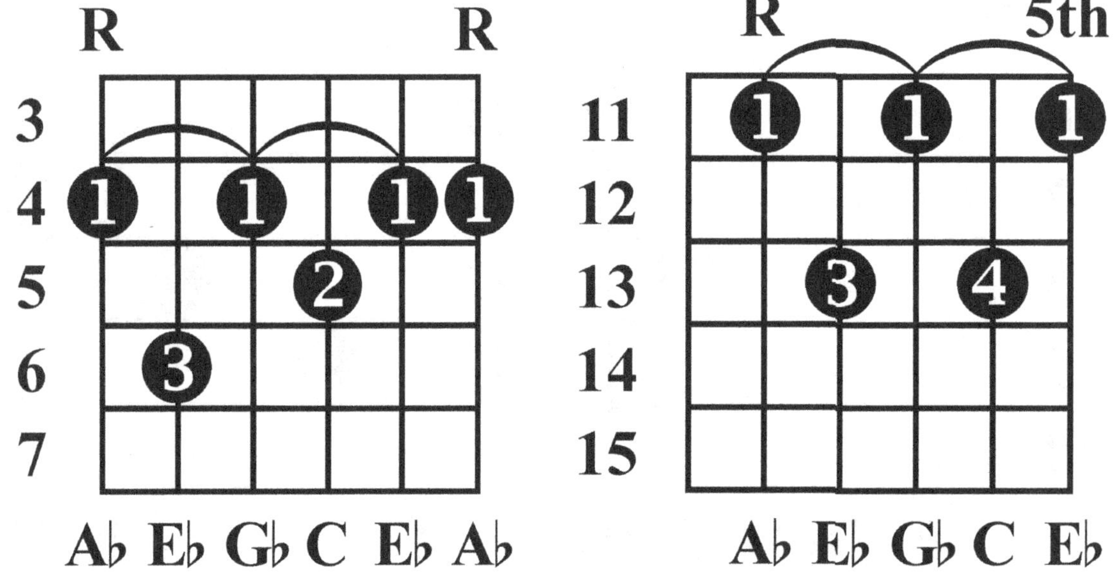

D♭7

R   R
Db F Cb Db

R   5th
Db Ab Cb F Ab
R   R
Db Ab Cb F Ab Db

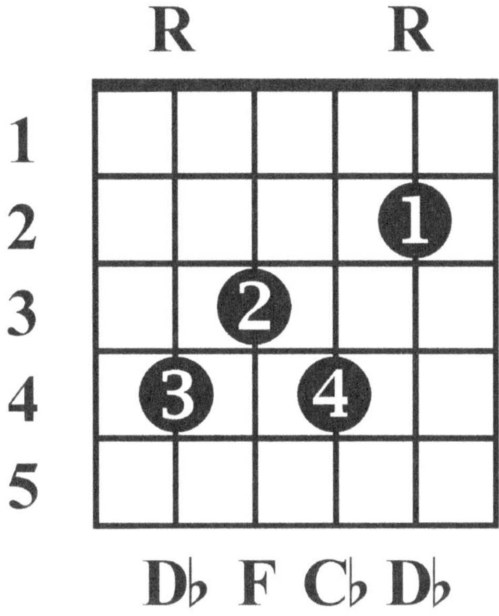

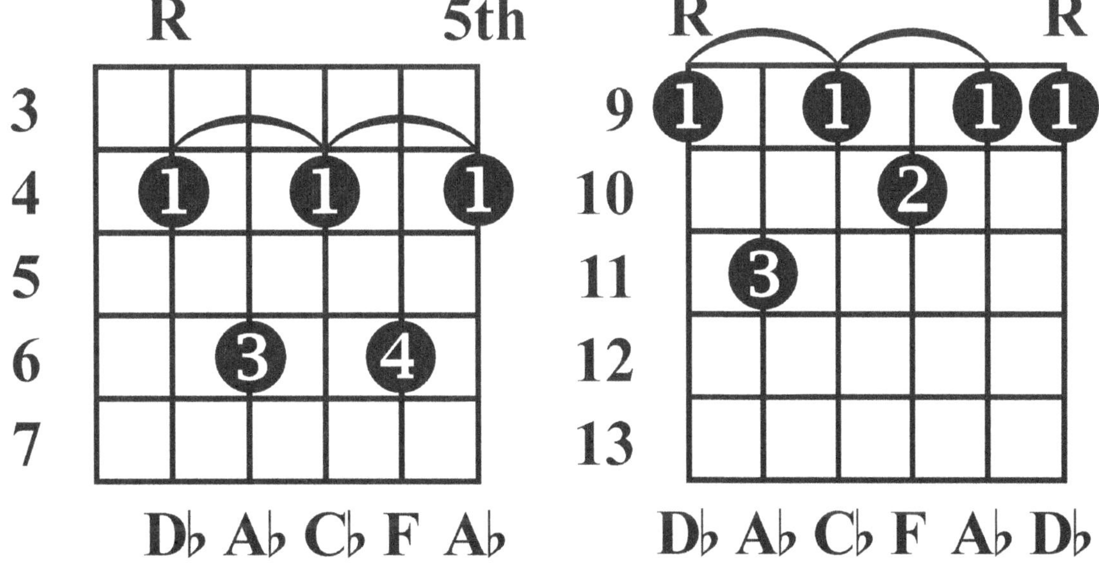

G♭7 / F♯7

R   R
1
2
3
4
5
G♭ D♭ F♭ B♭ D♭ G♭

R   3rd
3
4
5
6
7
G♭ D♭ F♭ B♭

R   5th
9
10
11
12
13
G♭ D♭ F♭ B♭ D♭

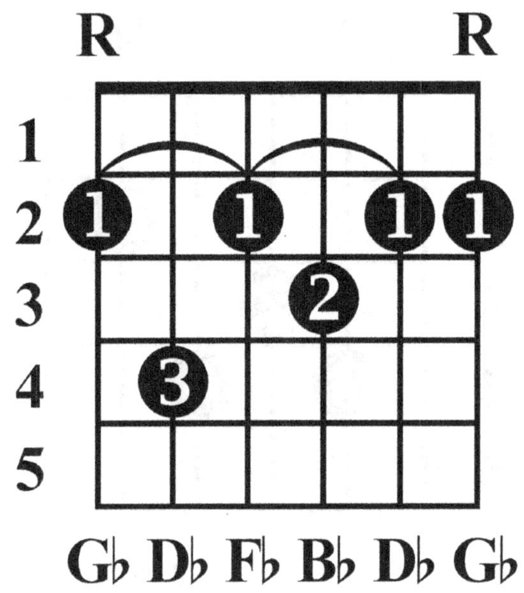

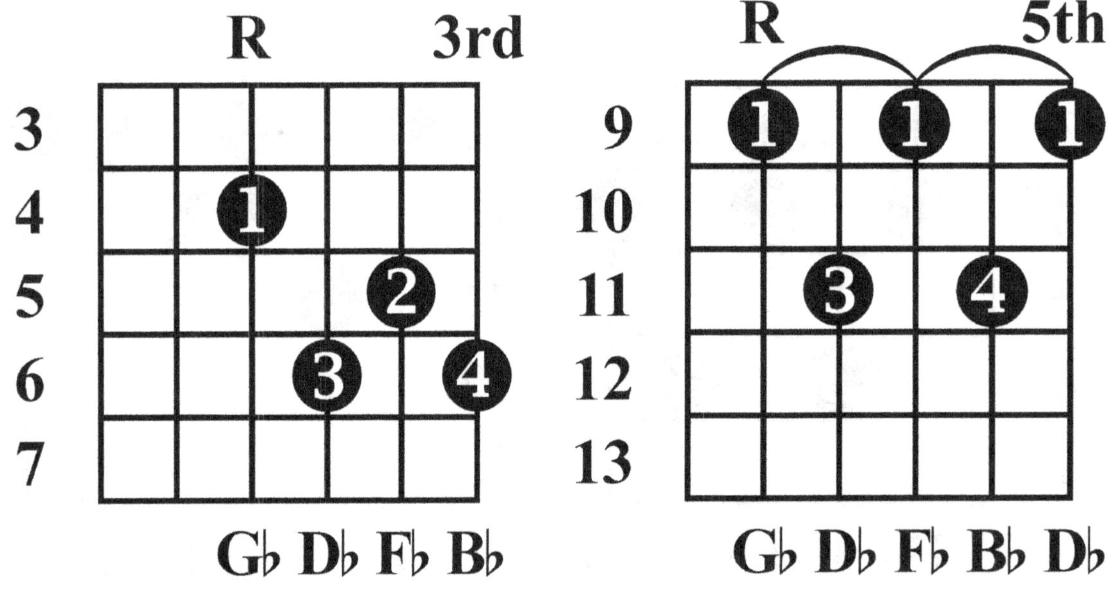

CMaj7

R
3rd
1
2
3
4
5
C E G B E

R
5th
3
4
5
6
7
C G B E G
R
M7th
7
8
9
10
11
C E G B

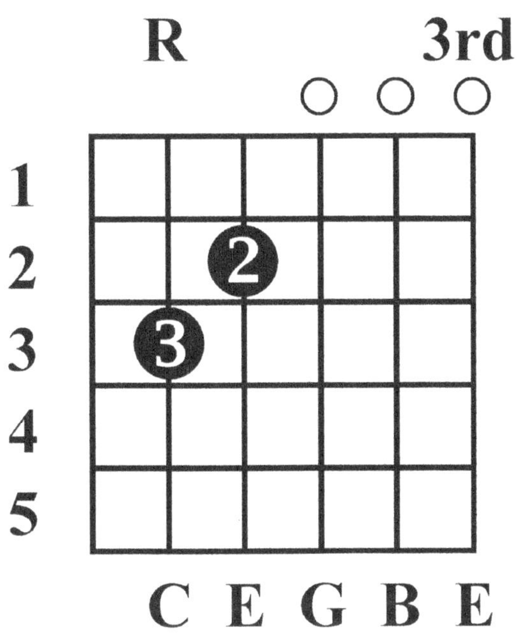

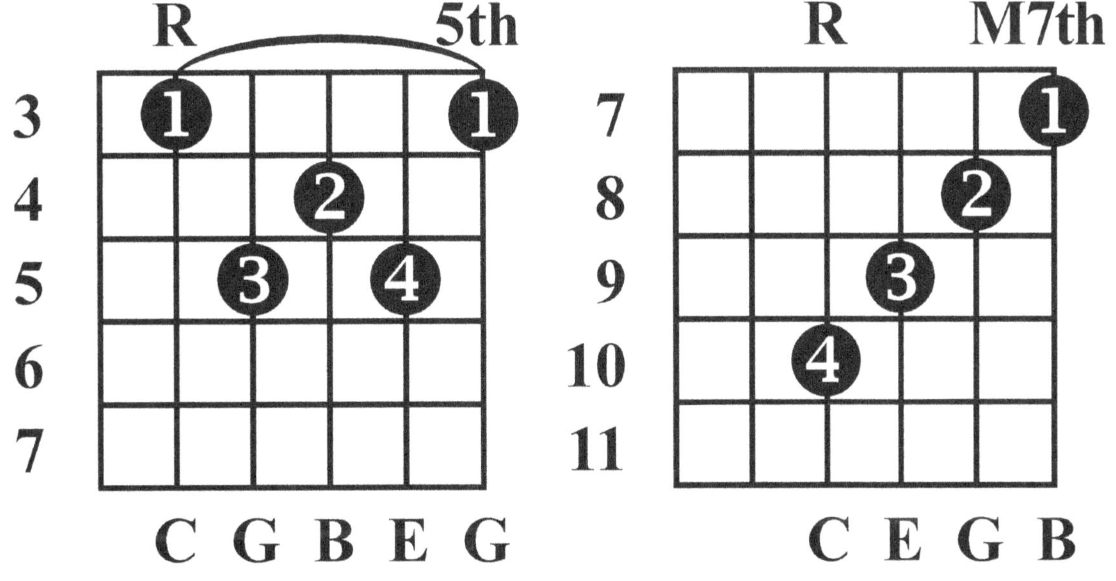

GMaj7

R
M7th
1
2
3
4
5
G B D G B F#

R
M7th
1
2
3
4
5
G B D F#
R
3rd
5
6
7
8
9
G D F# B

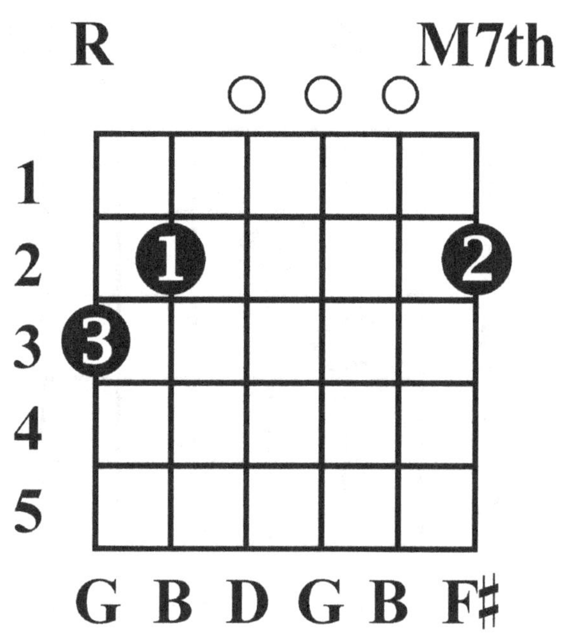

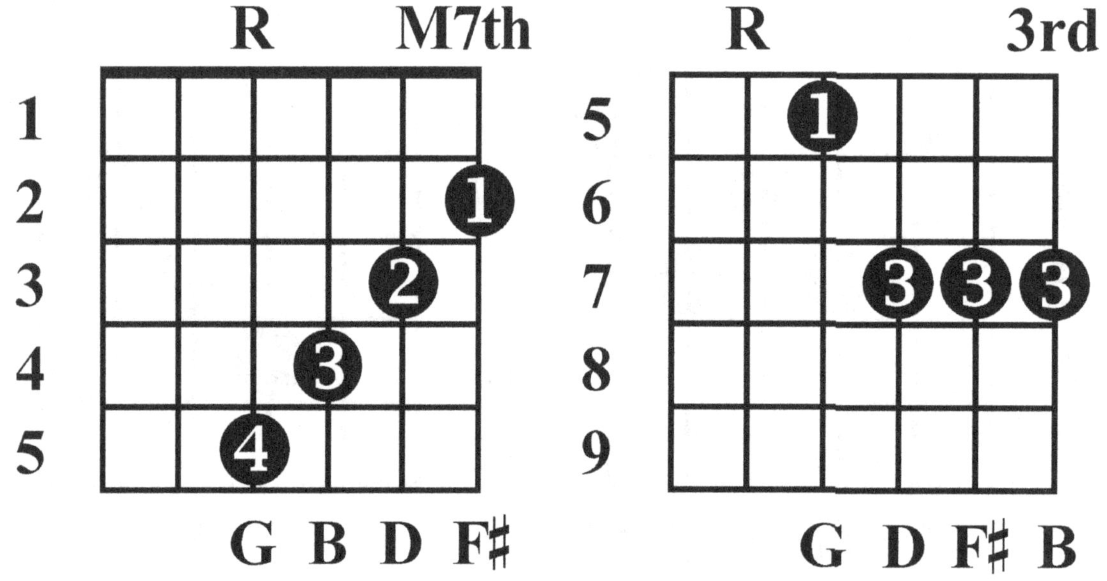

DMaj7

R   3rd
D A C# F#

R   5th
D A C# F# A

5th   M7th
A D F# C#

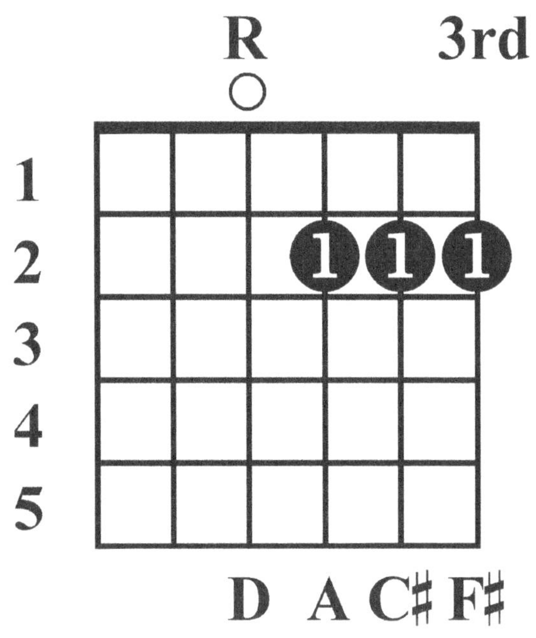

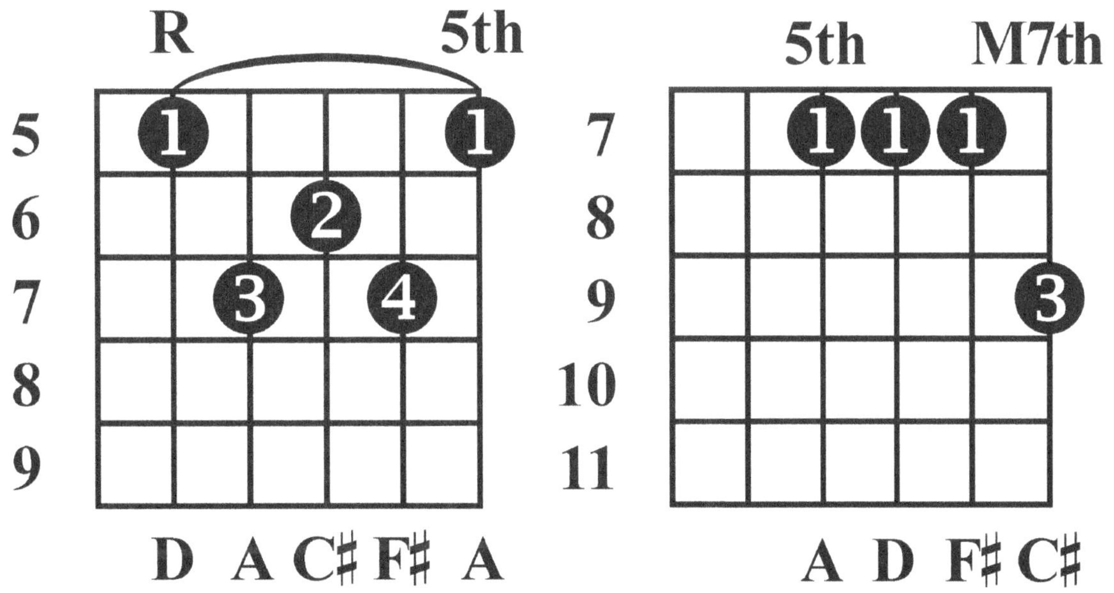

AMaj7

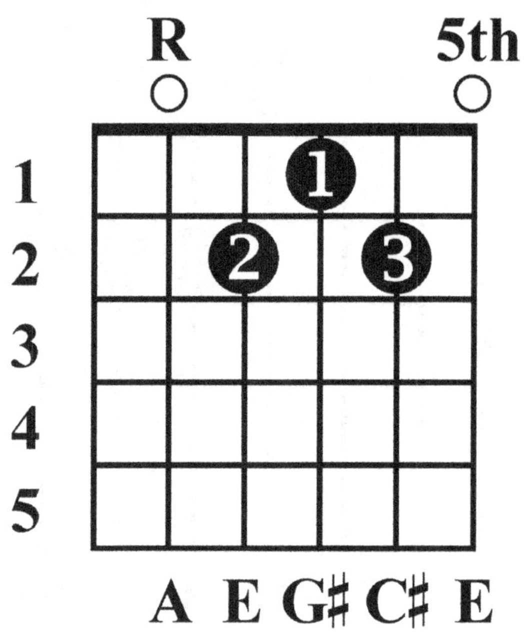

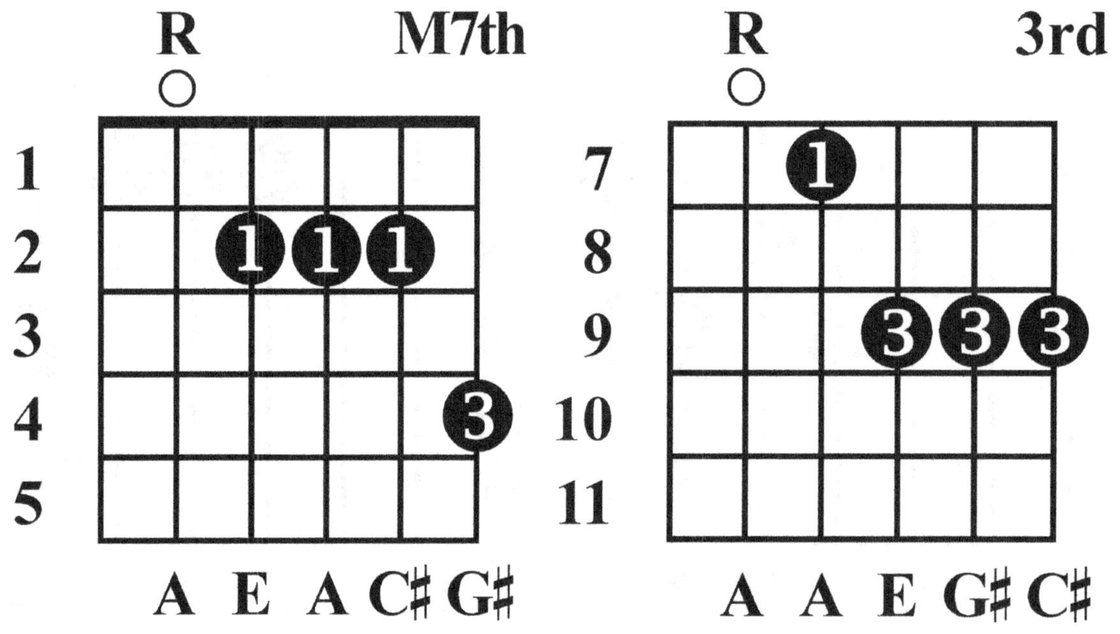

E, B, F, B♭Maj7

EMaj7

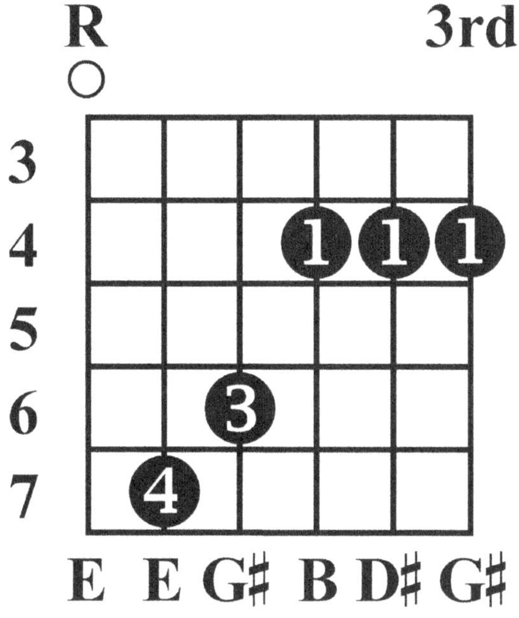

BMaj7

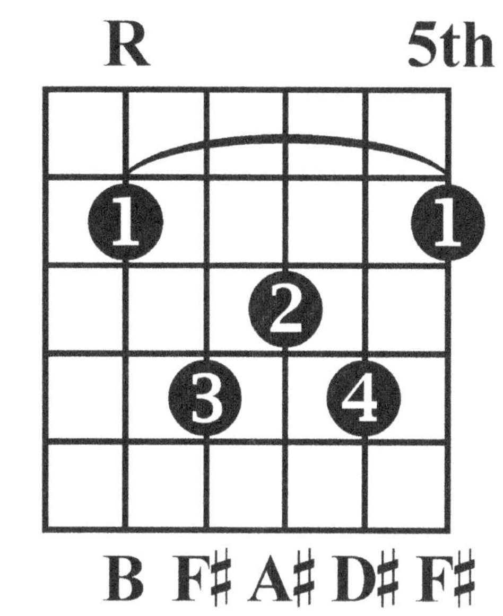

FMaj7

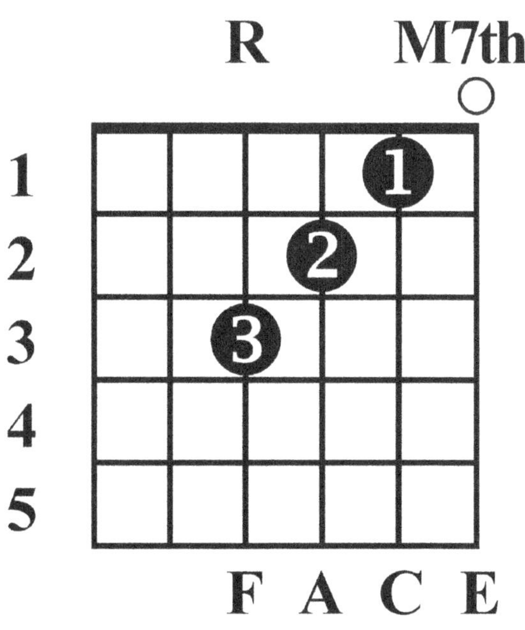

B♭Maj7

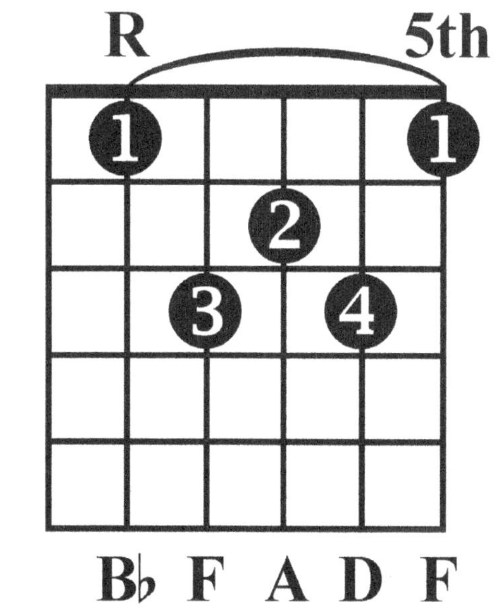

E♭, A♭, D♭, G♭/ F♯ Maj7

E♭Maj7　　　A♭Maj7

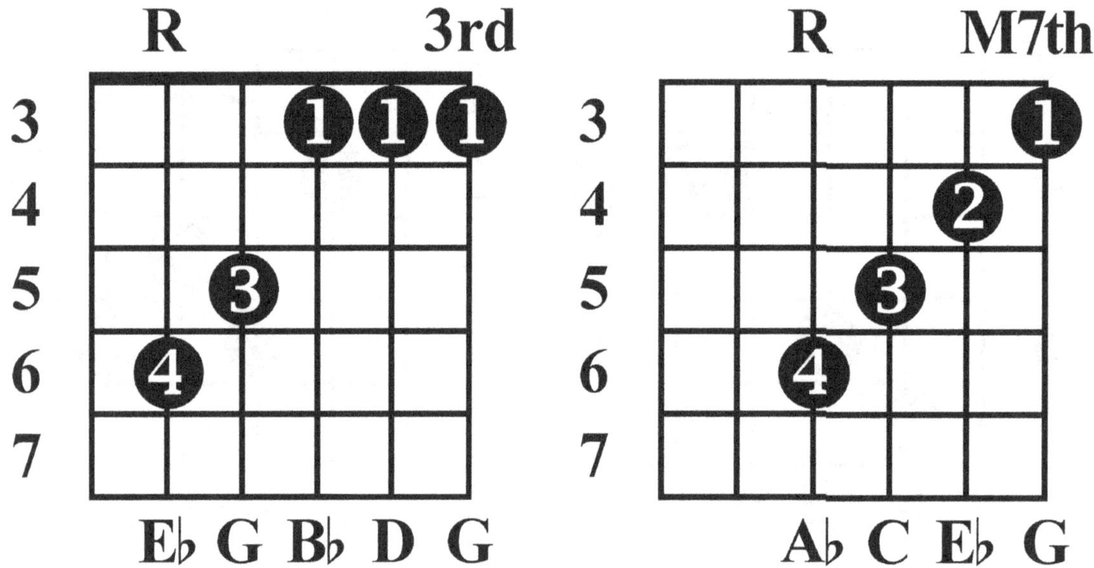

D♭Maj7　　　G♭/ F♯Maj7

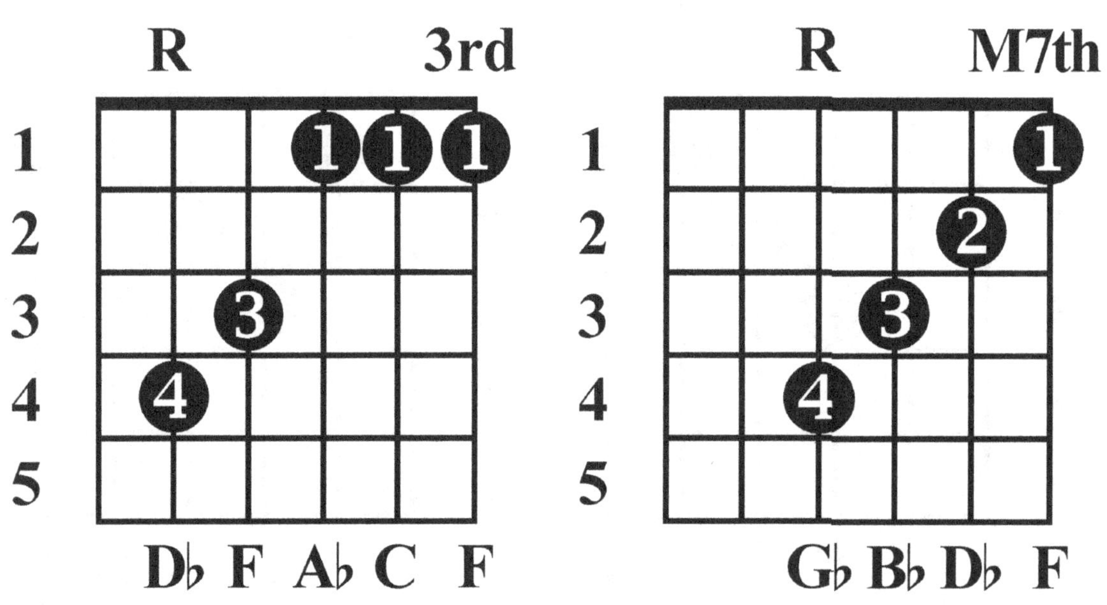

C6

R   3rd
C E A C E

5th   6th
G C E A
R   ⊗   R
C G   E A C

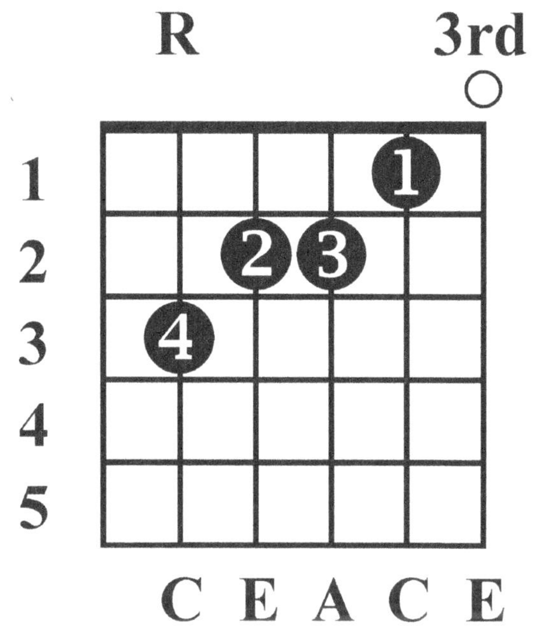

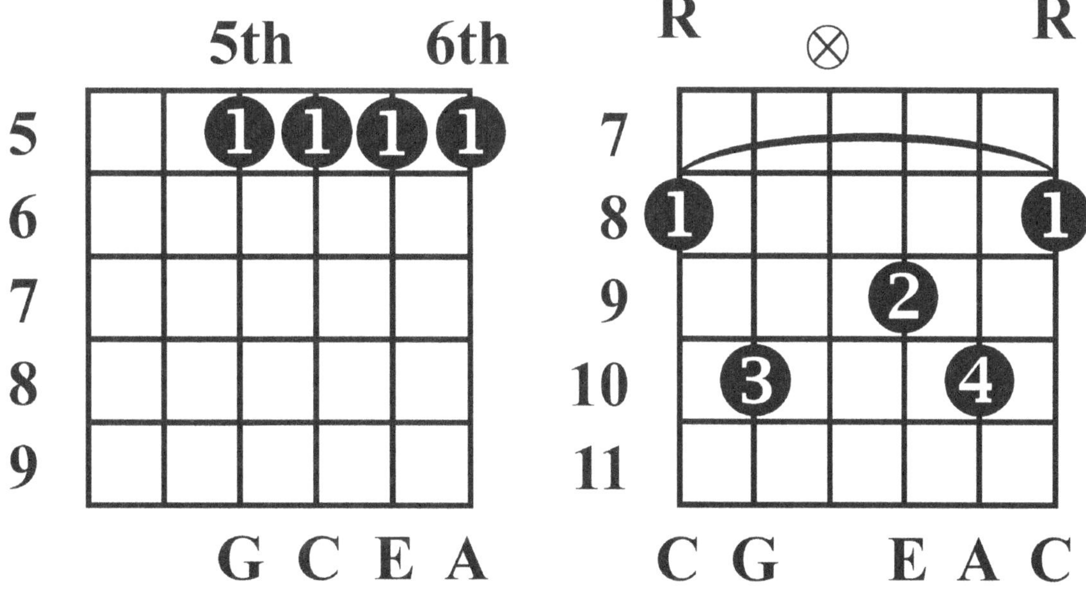

G6

R
6th
1
2
3
4
5
G B D E

R
R
R
3rd
3
4
5
6
7
5
6
7
8
9
G D B E G
G D E B

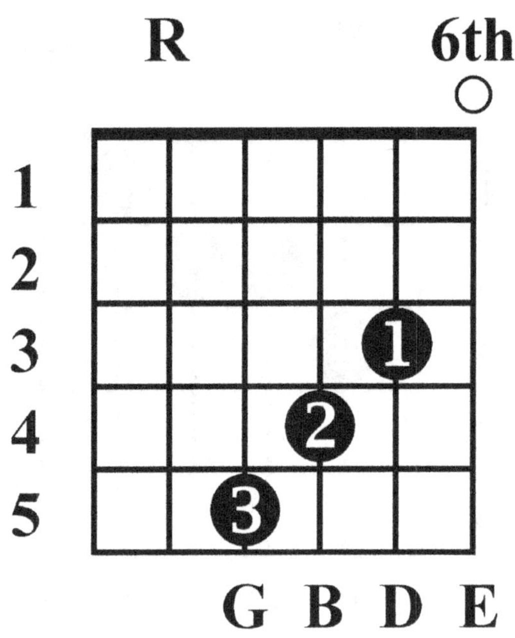

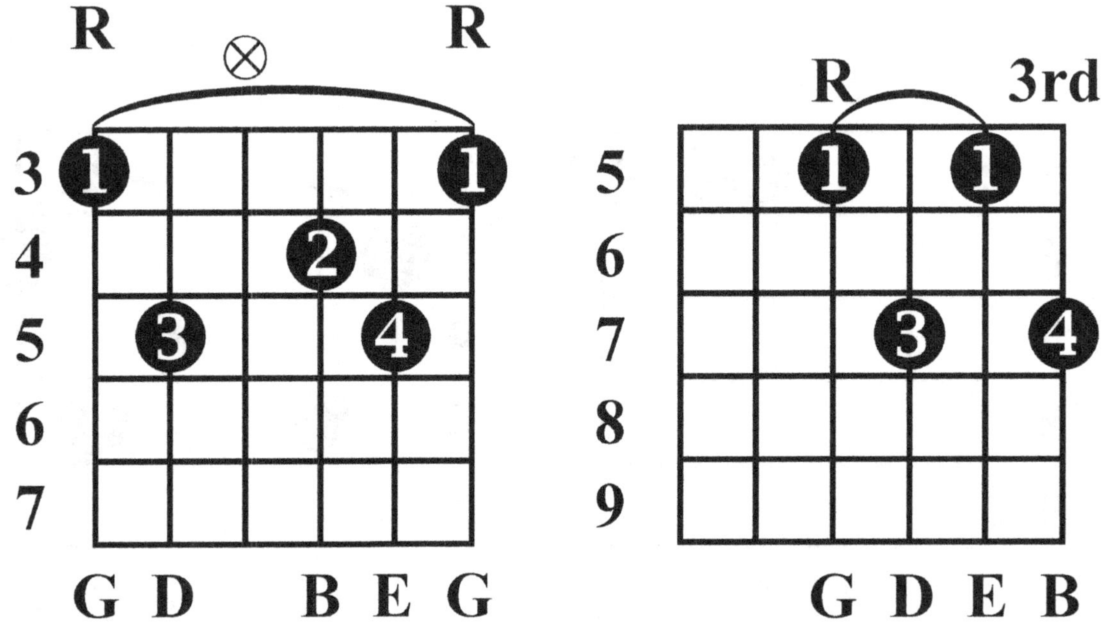

D6

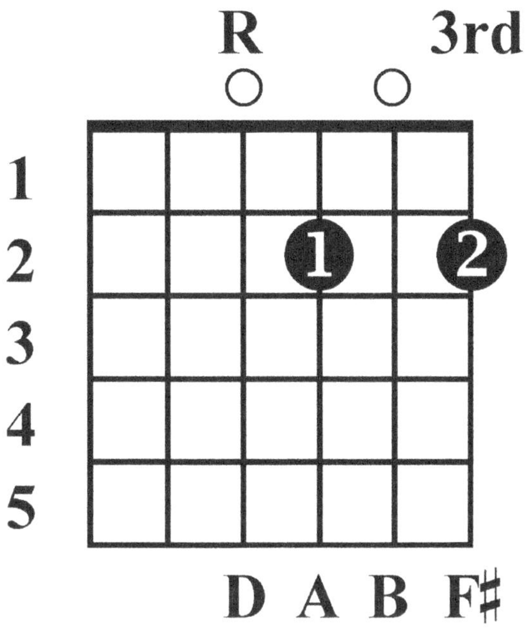

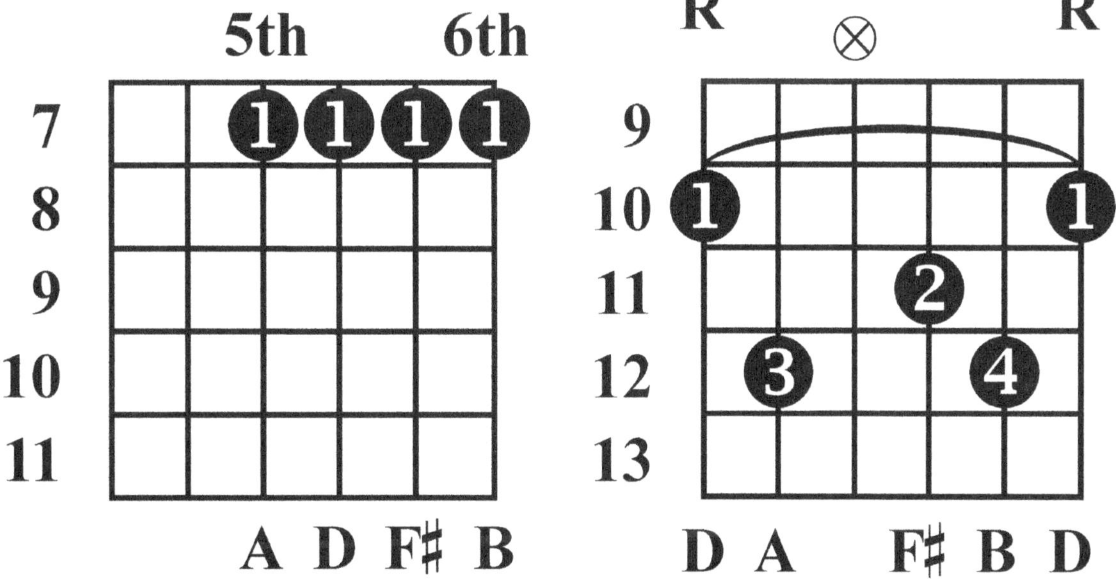

A6

R
6th
A E A C# F#

R
R
A F# C# E A
R
R
A E C# F# A

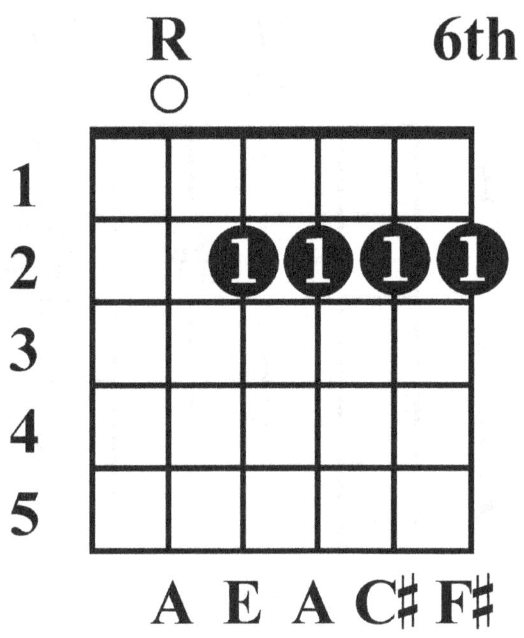

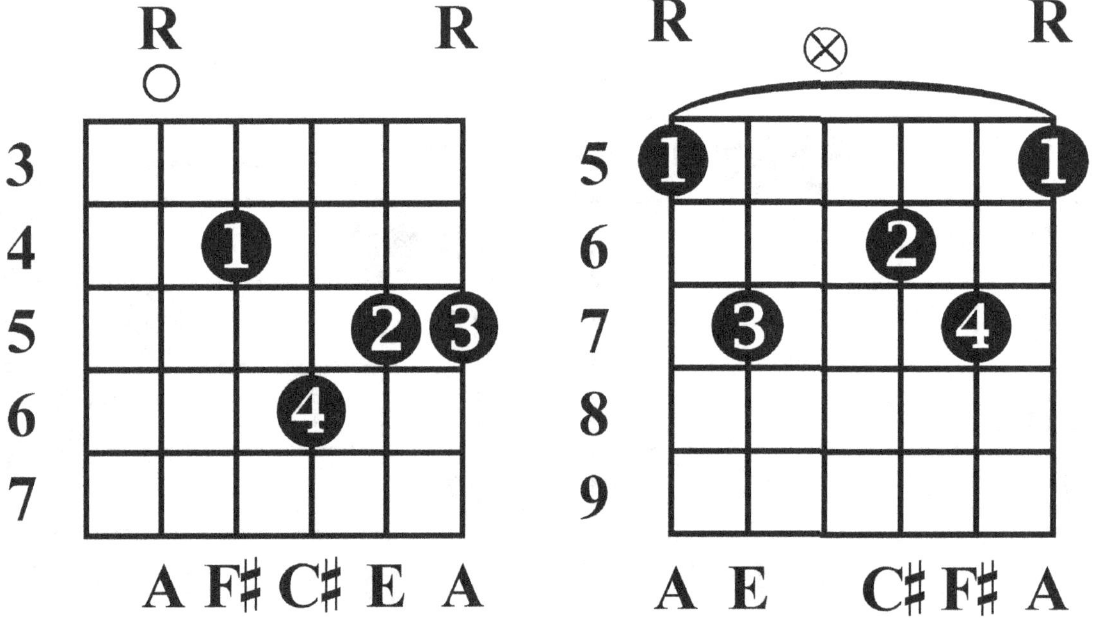

E, B, F, B♭6

E6
R R
1 2 3 4 5
E B E G# C# E

B6
R 6th
1 2 3 4 5
B F# B D# G#

F6
R R
1 2 3 4 5
F C A D E

B♭6
R 3rd
1 2 3 4 5
B♭ F G D

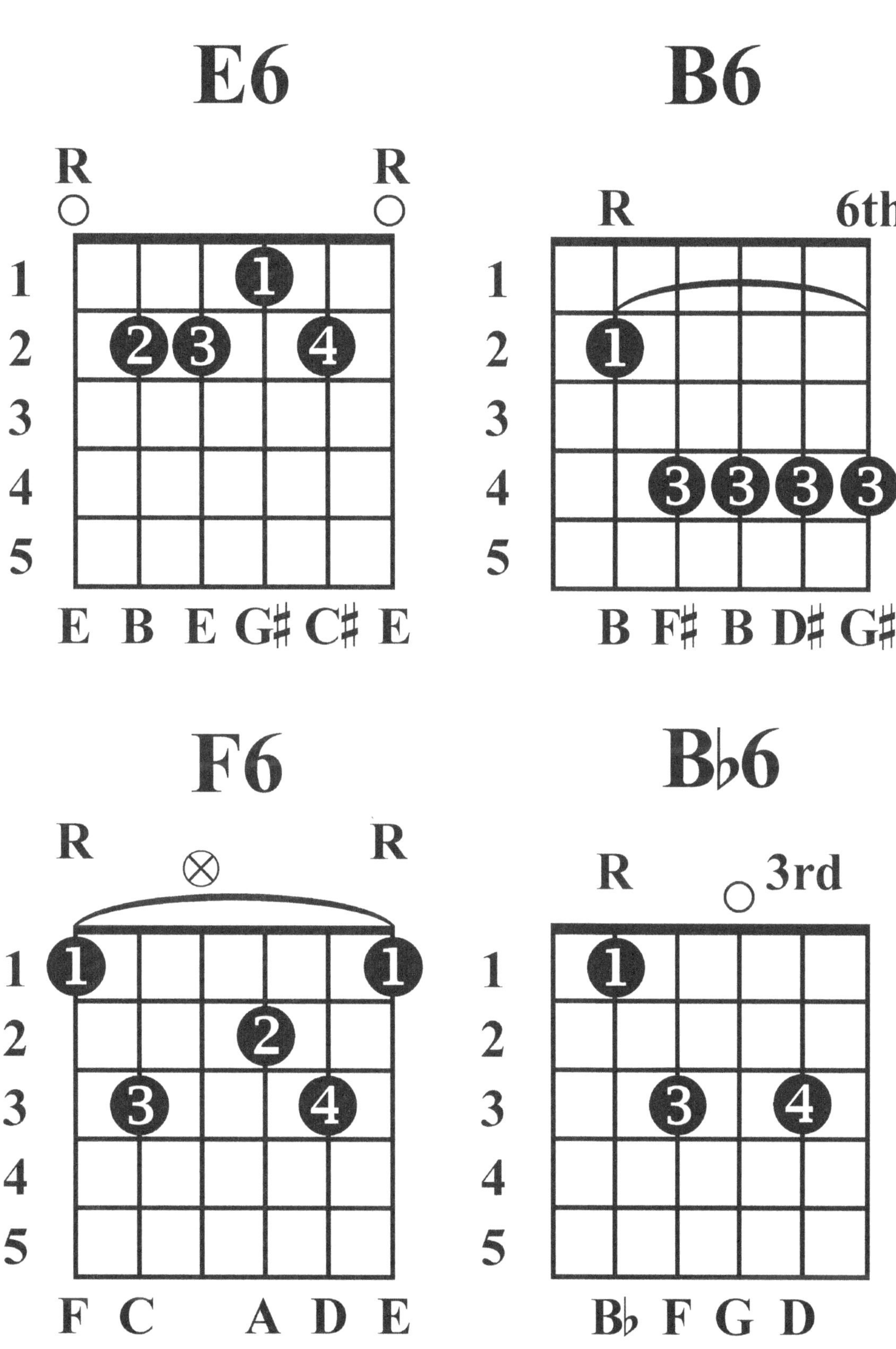

E♭, A♭, D♭, G♭ / F♯6

E♭6

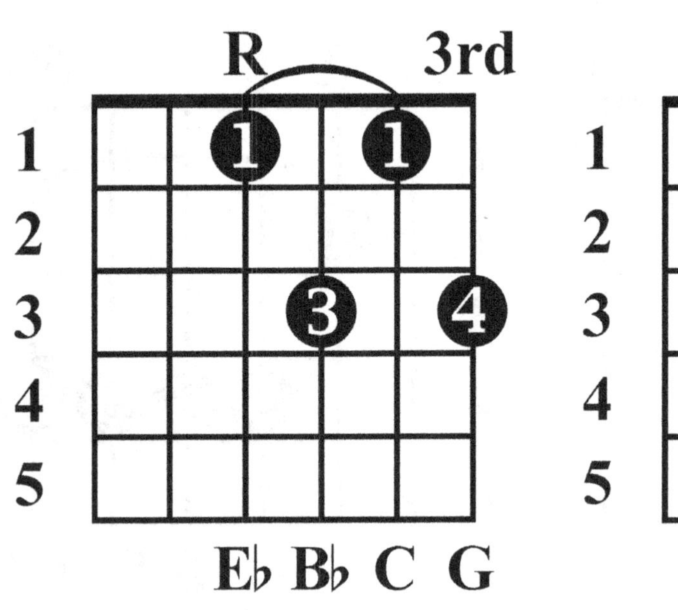

A♭6

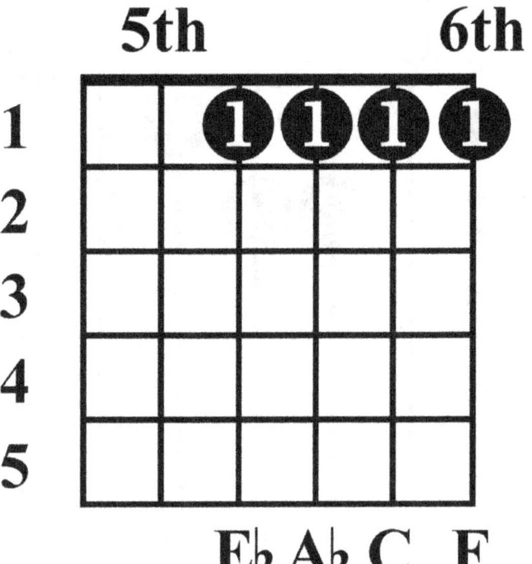

D♭6

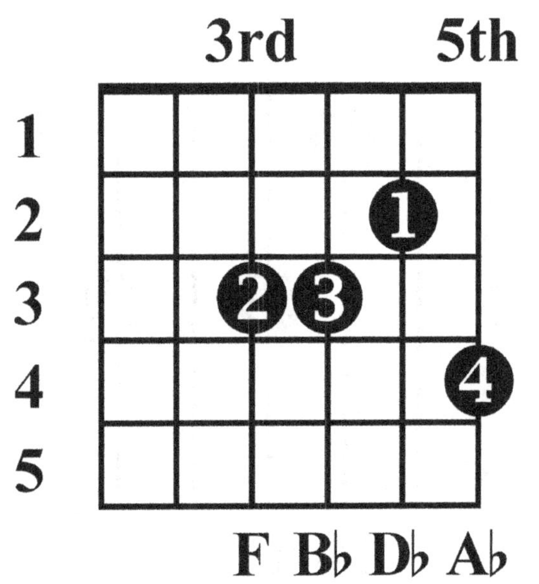

G♭6 / F♯6

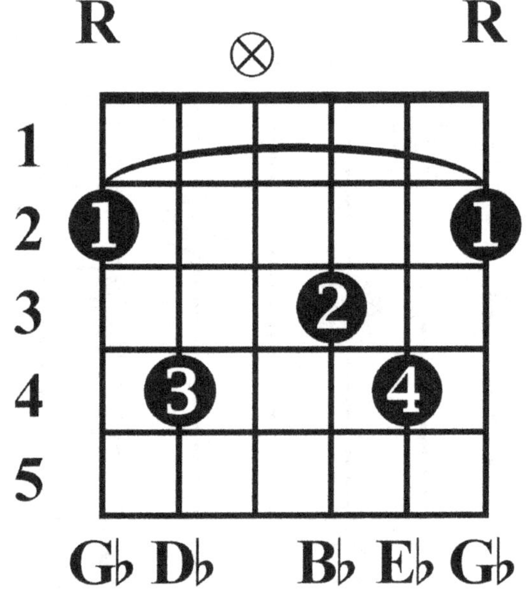

Cm7

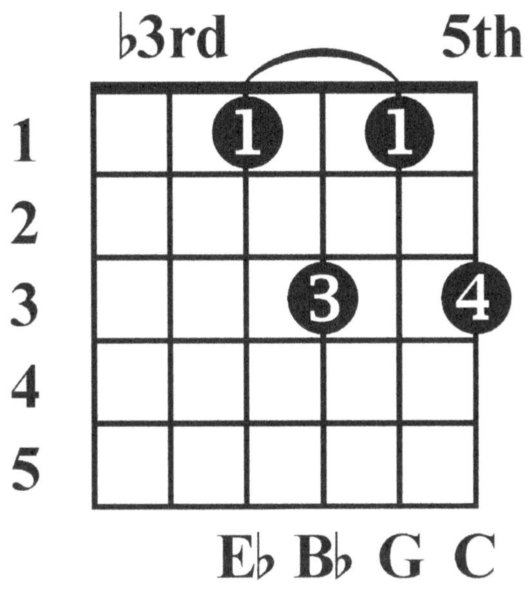

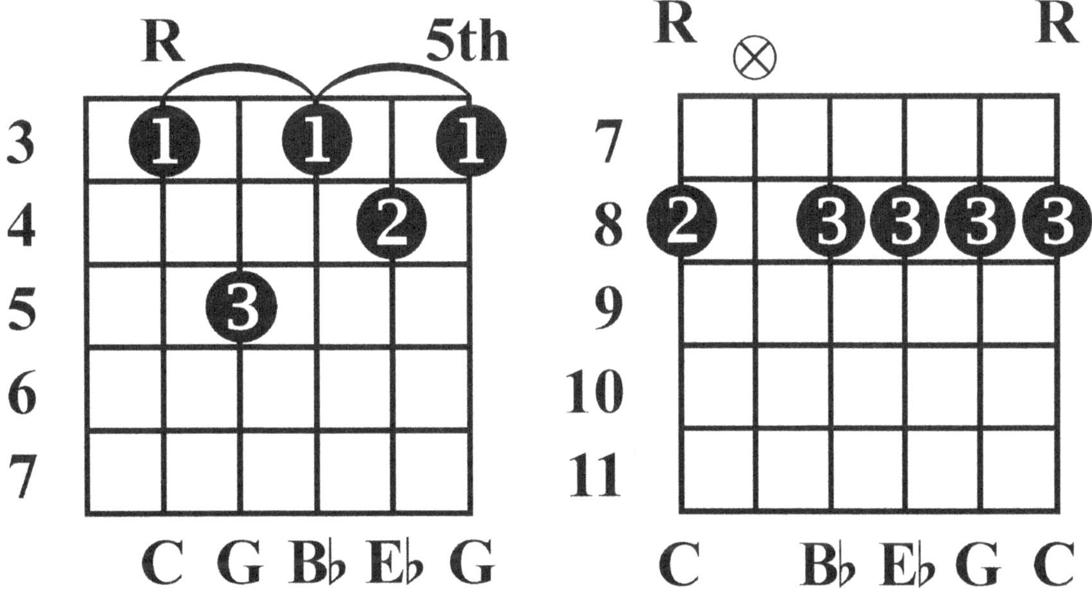

Gm7

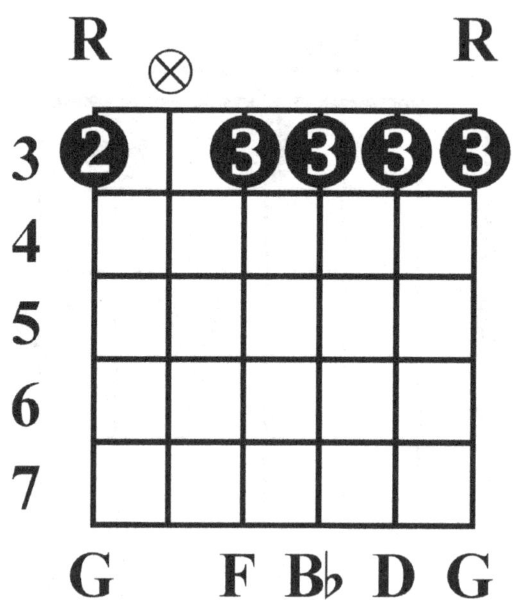

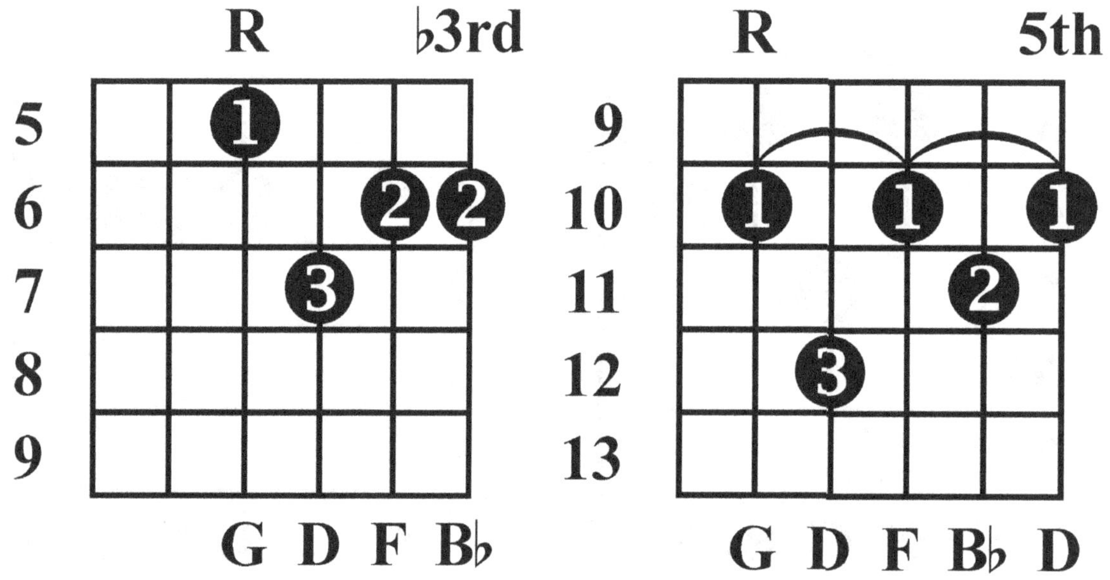

Dm7

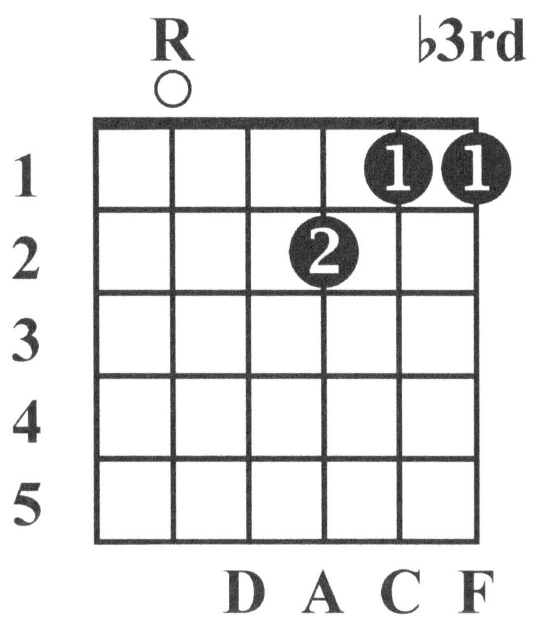

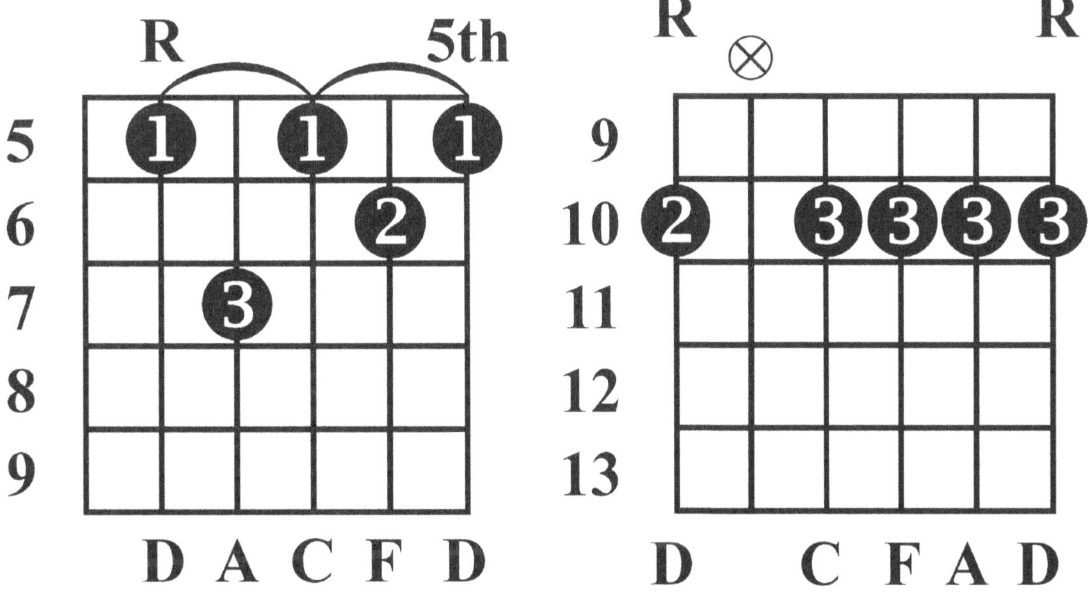

Am7

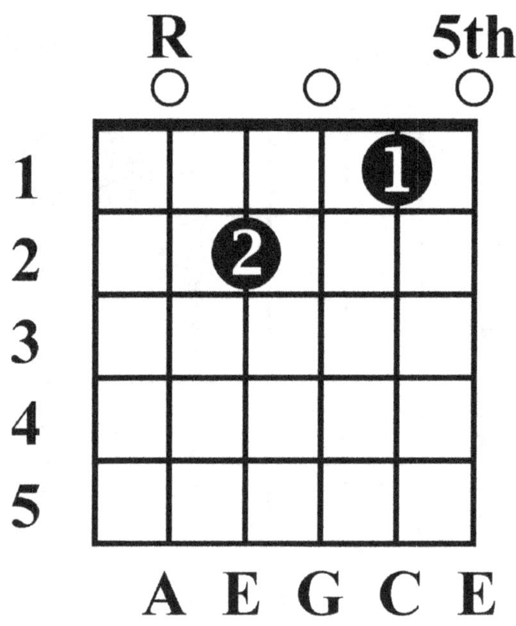

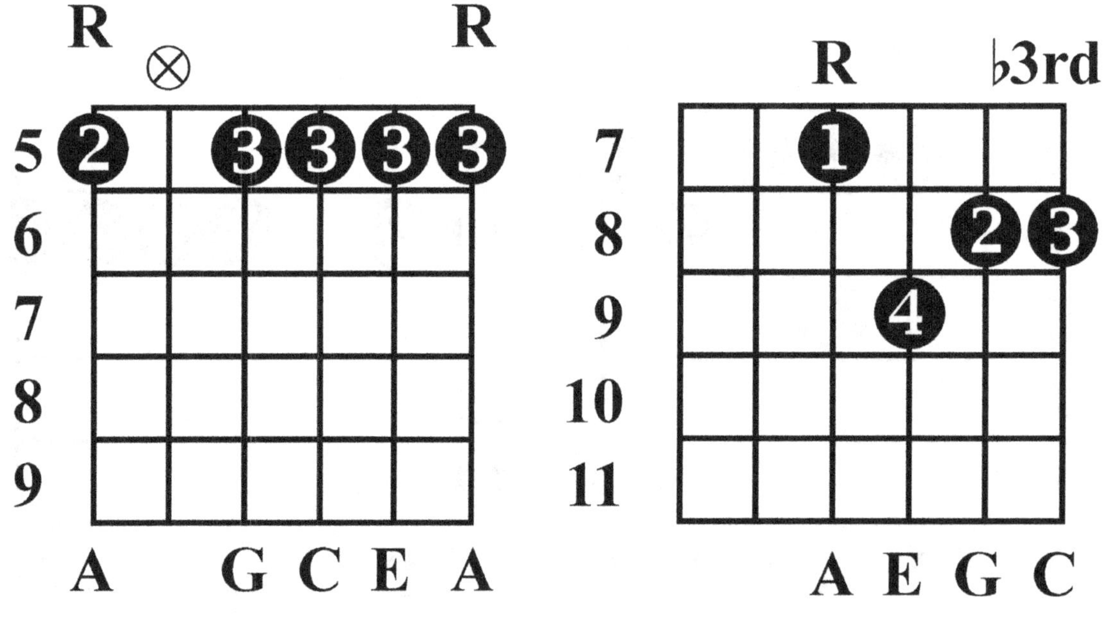

E, B, F, B♭m7

Em7
R R
E B E G D B
Bm7
R 5th
B F♯ A D F♯
Fm7
R 5th
F C E♭ A♭ C
B♭m7
R 5th
B♭ F A♭ D♭ F

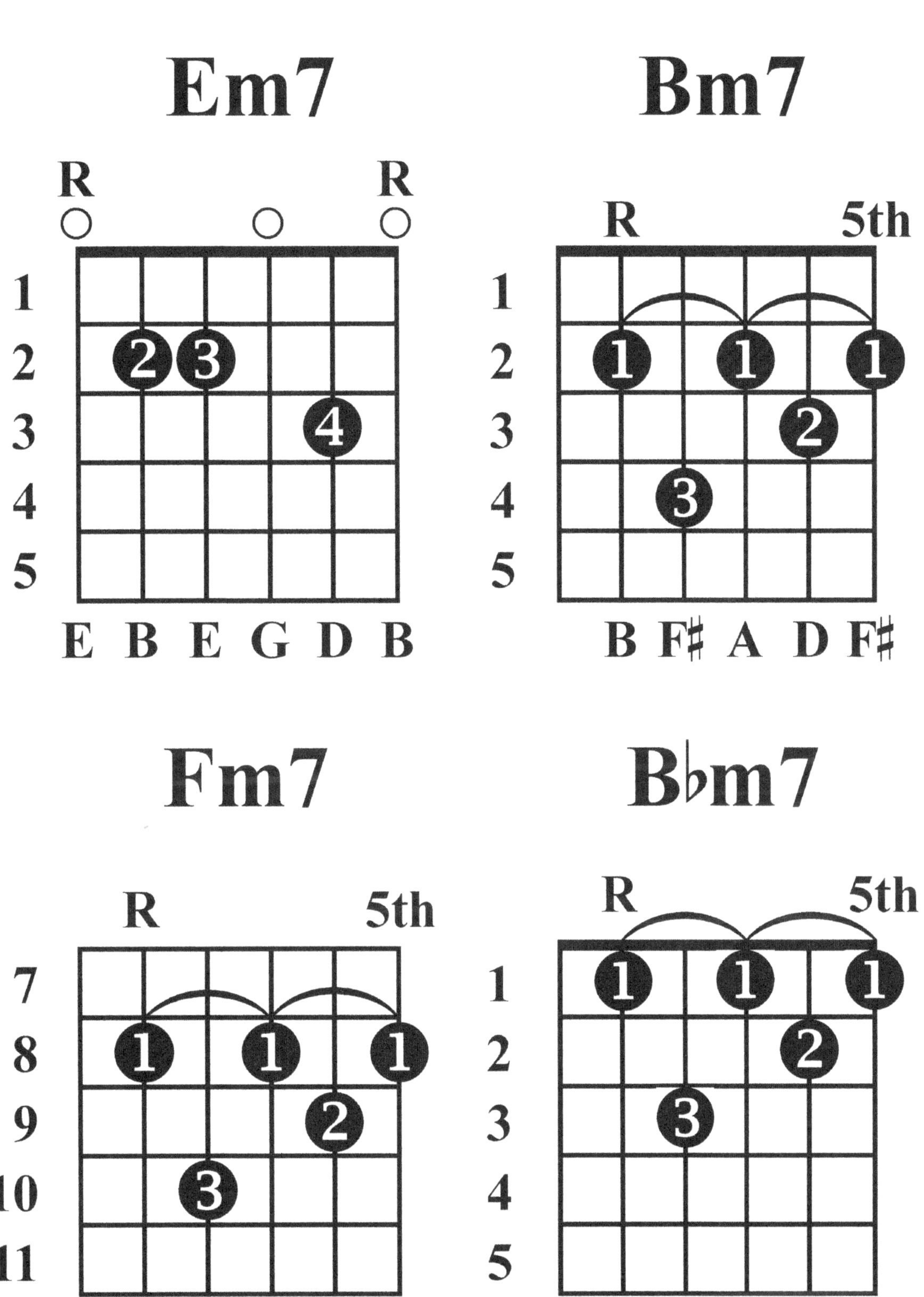

E♭, A♭, D♭, G♭ / F#m7

E♭m7

A♭m7

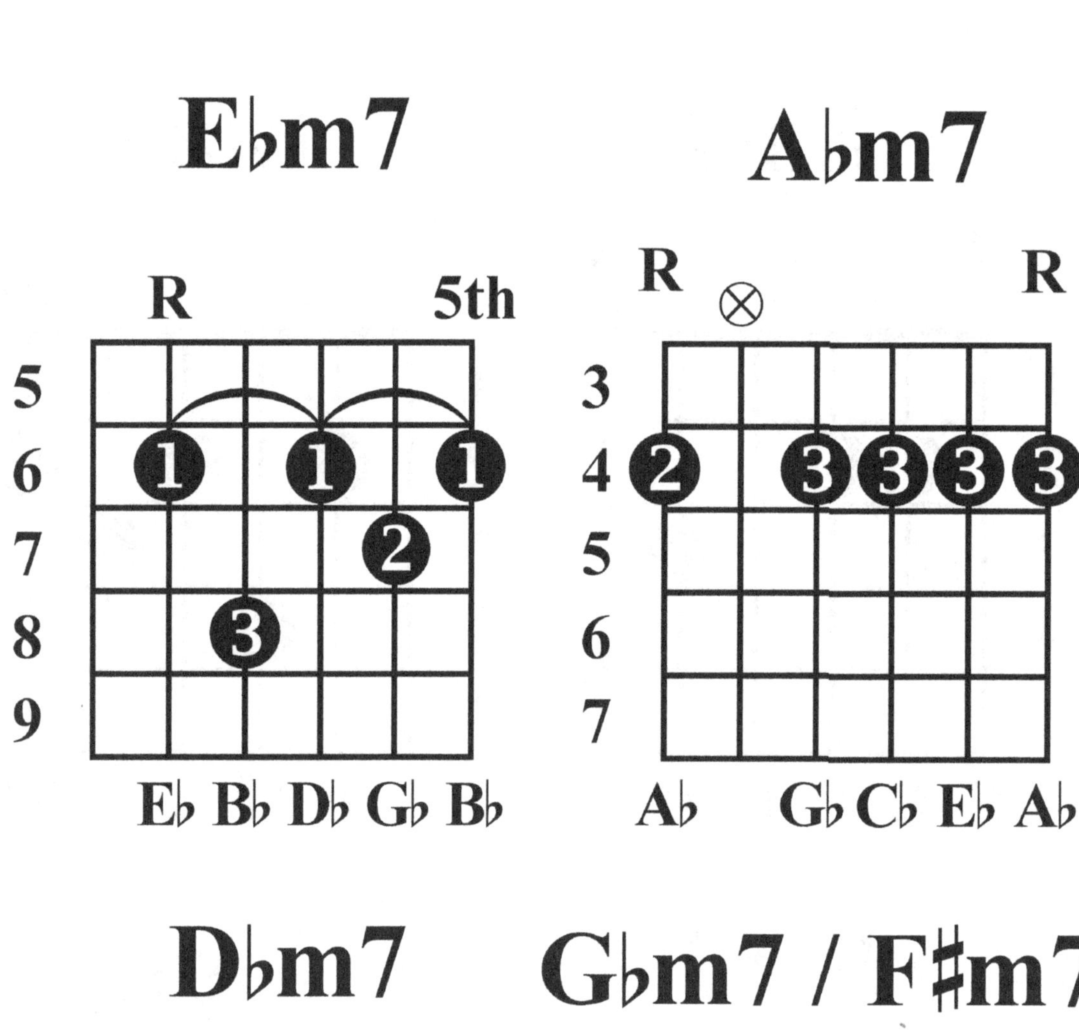

D♭m7

G♭m7 / F#m7

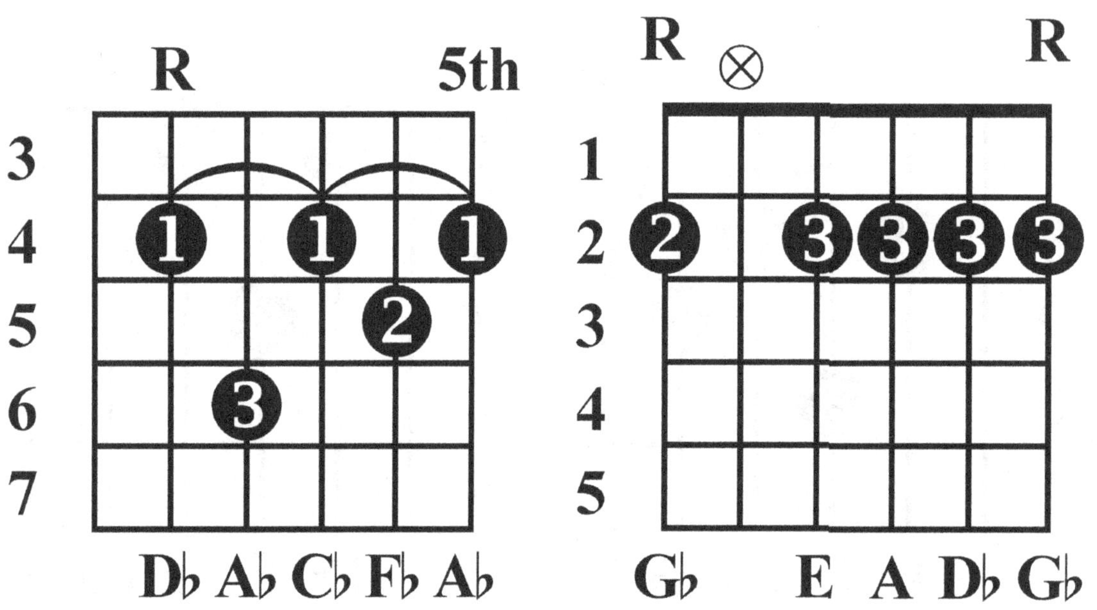

Cadd9

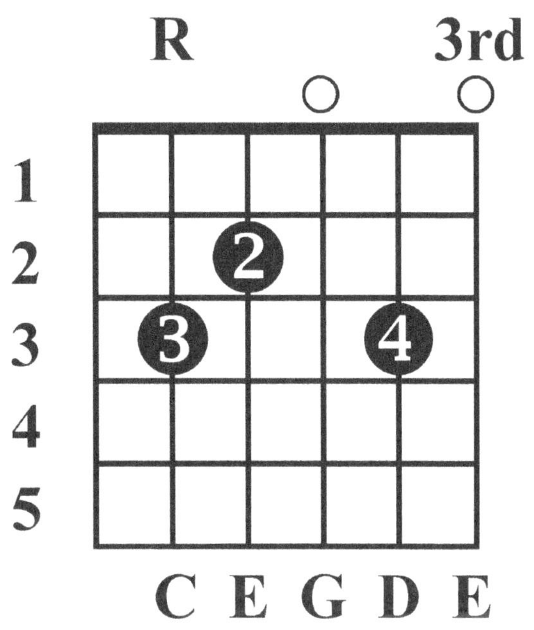

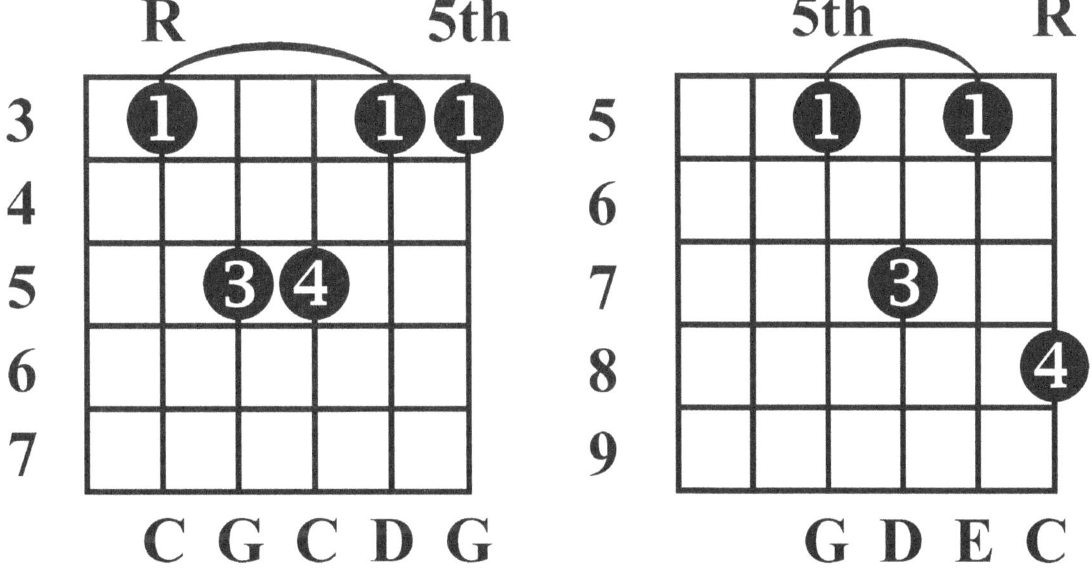

Gadd9

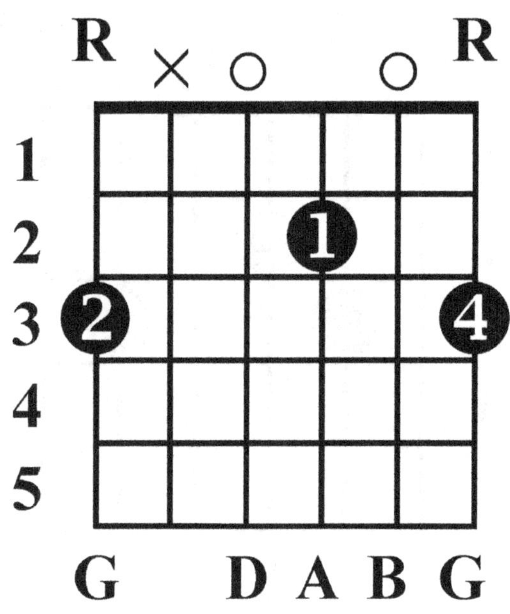

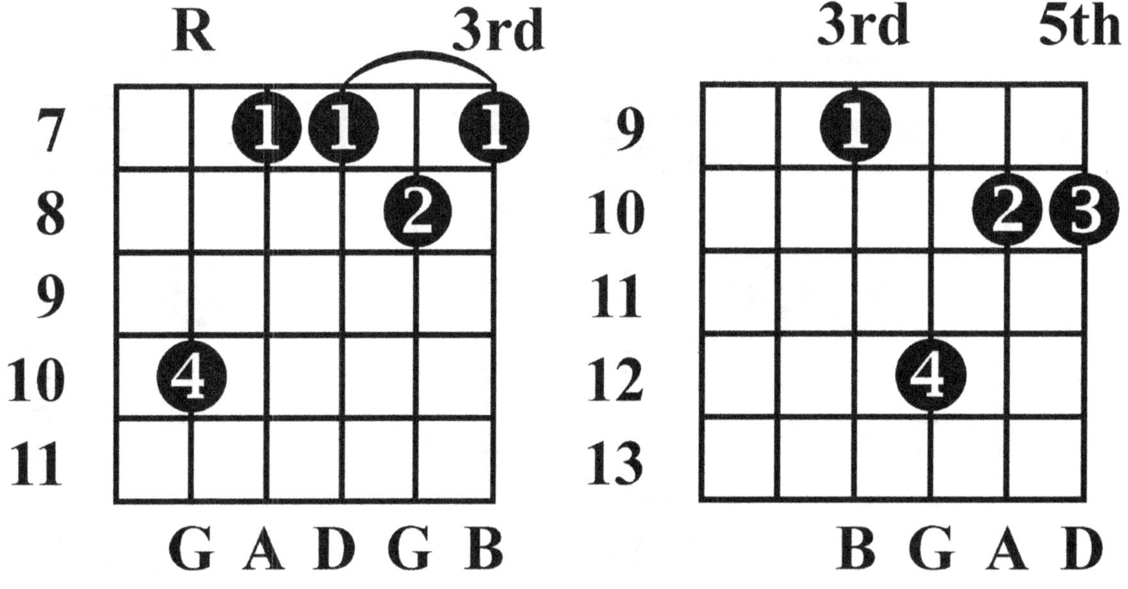

Dadd9

R
5th
1
2
3
4
5
1
3
D A D E

R
5th
5
6
7
8
9
1
1 1
3 4
D A D E A
5th
R
7
8
9
10
11
1 1
3
4
A E F♯ D

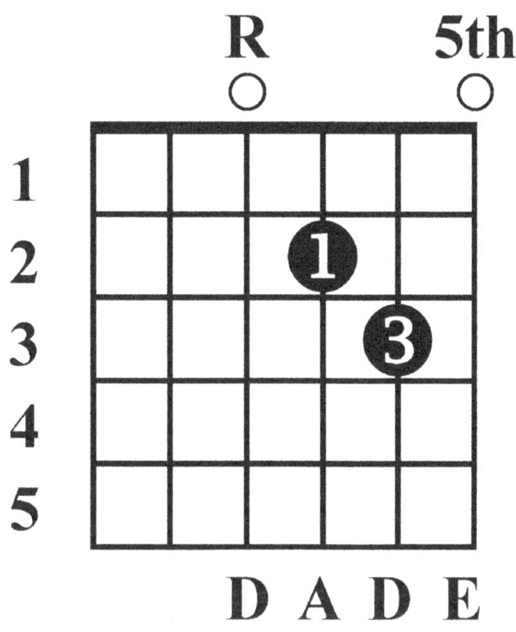

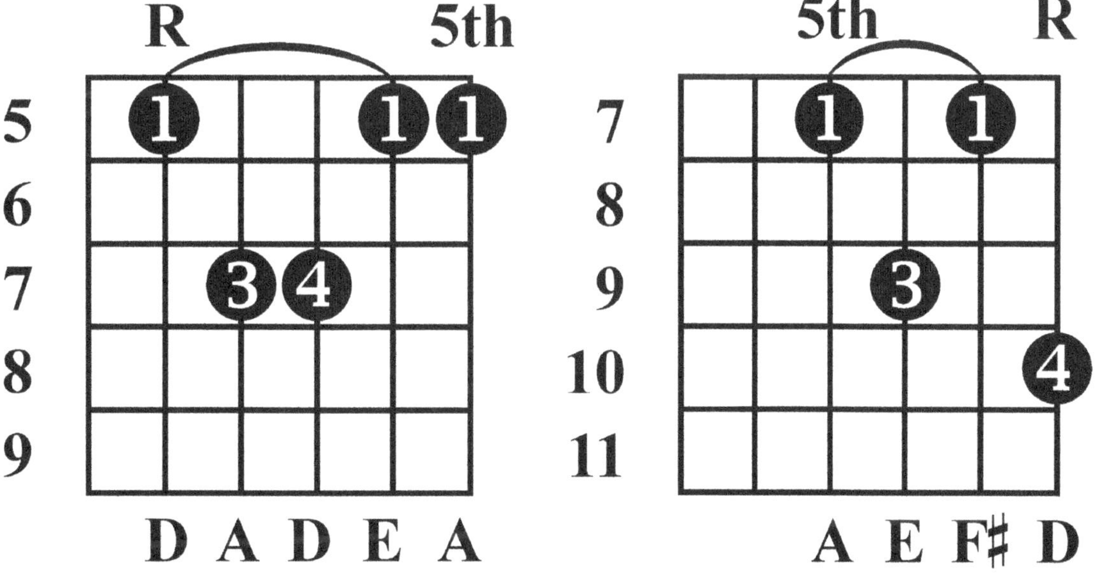

Aadd9

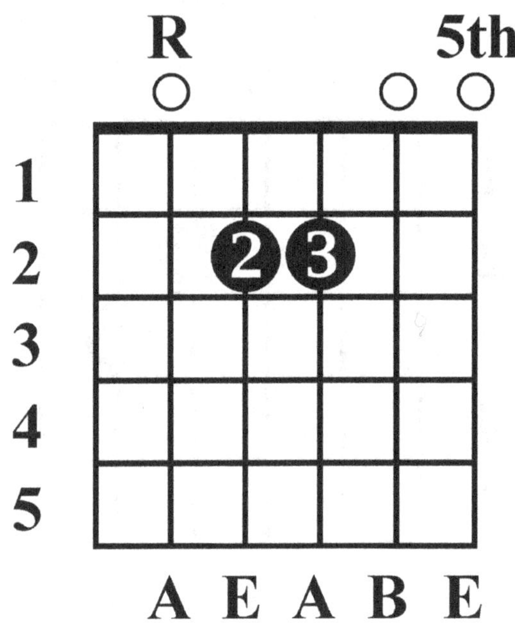

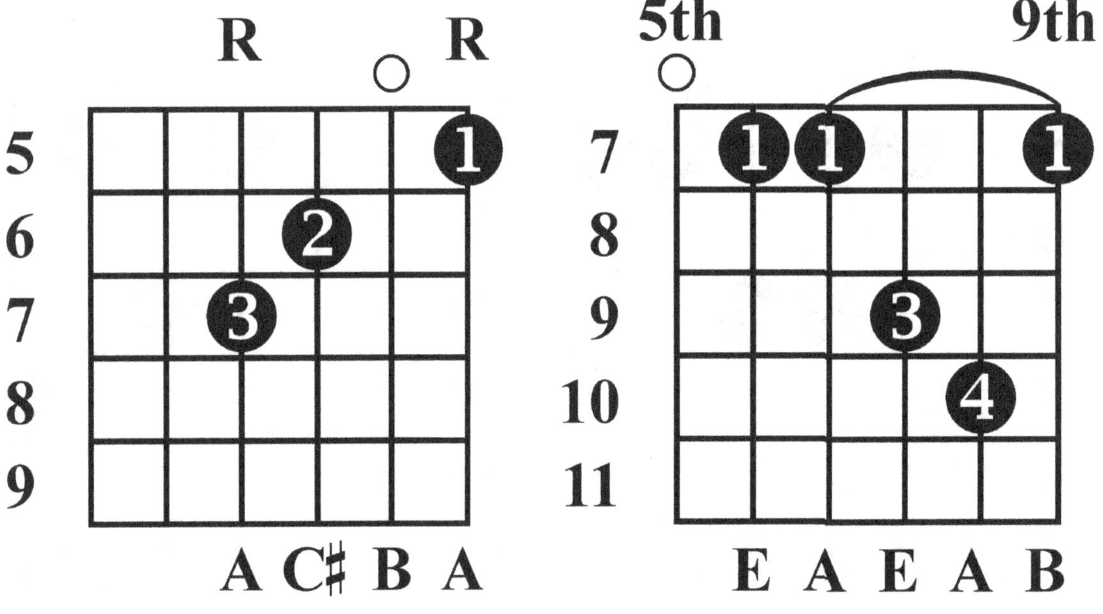

E, B, F, B♭add9

Eadd9

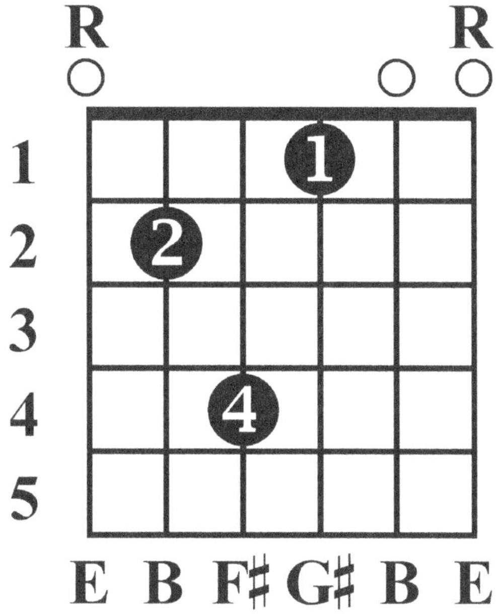

Badd9

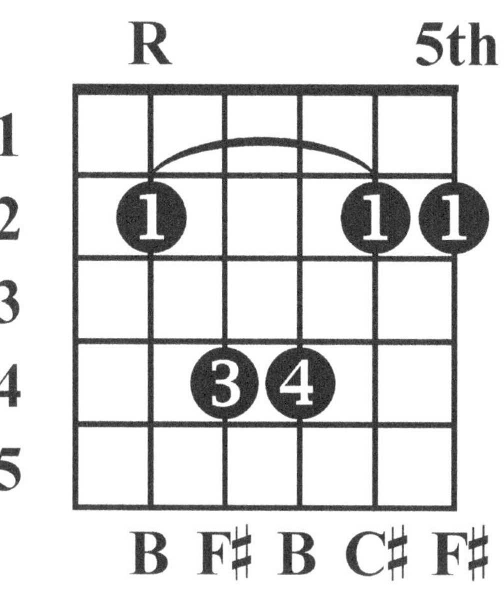

Fadd9

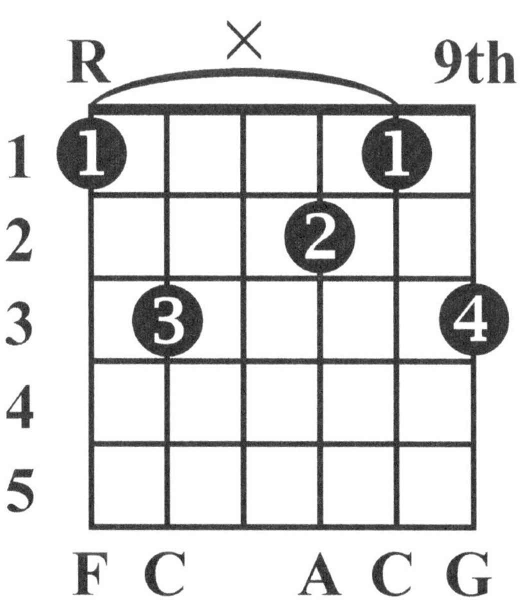

B♭add9

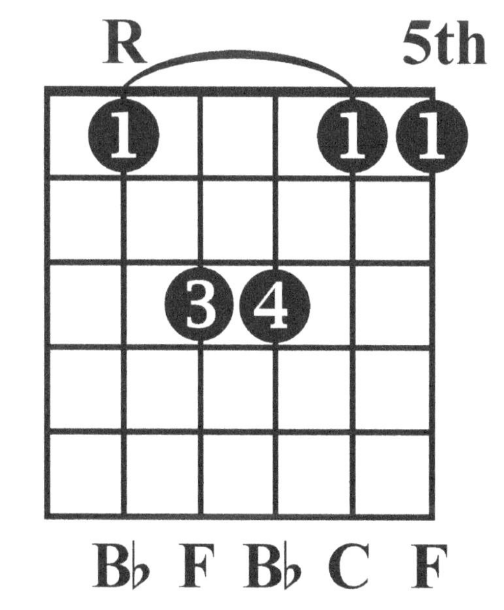

E♭, A♭, D♭, G♭/F♯add9

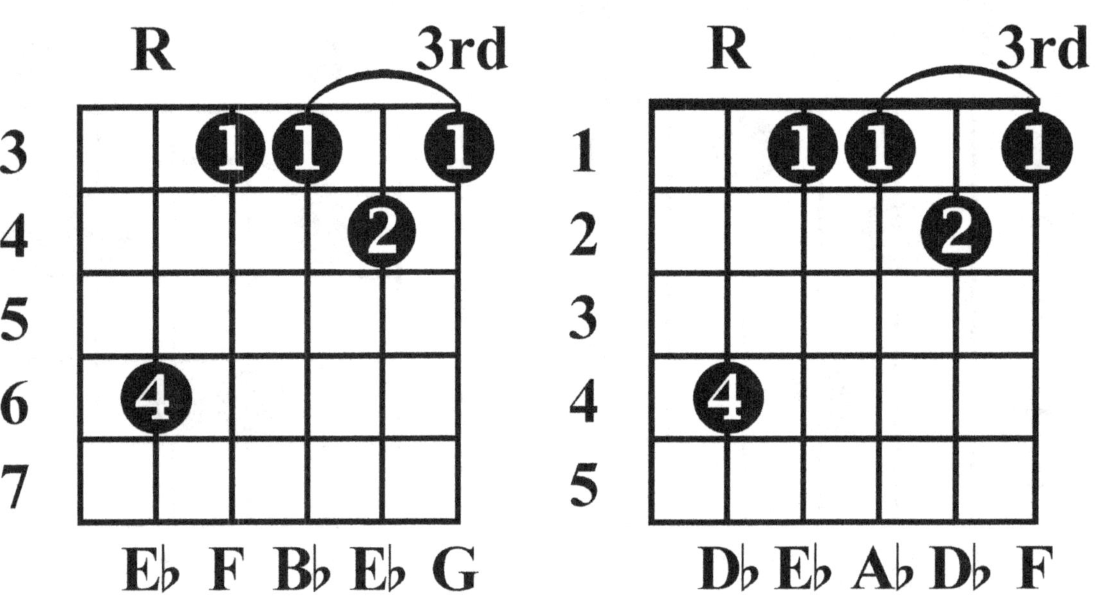

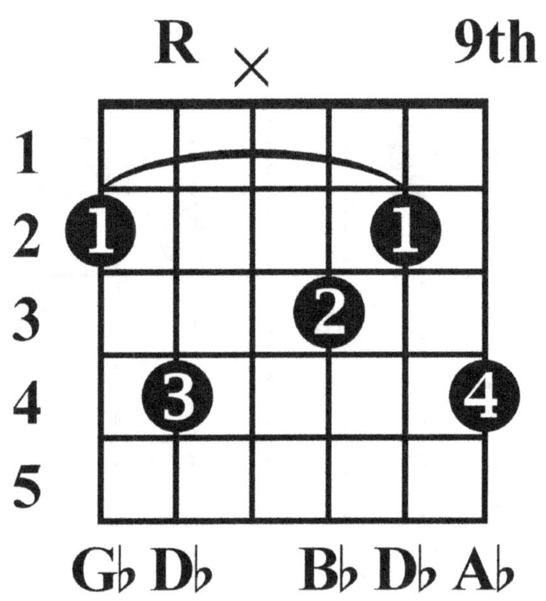

Cm add9

R 9th
1
2
3
C E♭ G D

5th R
4
5
6
7
8
G D E♭ C
b3rd R
5
6
7
8
9
E♭ G D G C

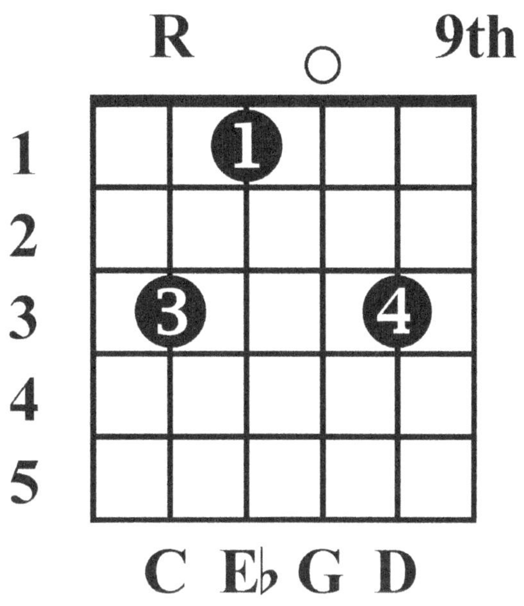

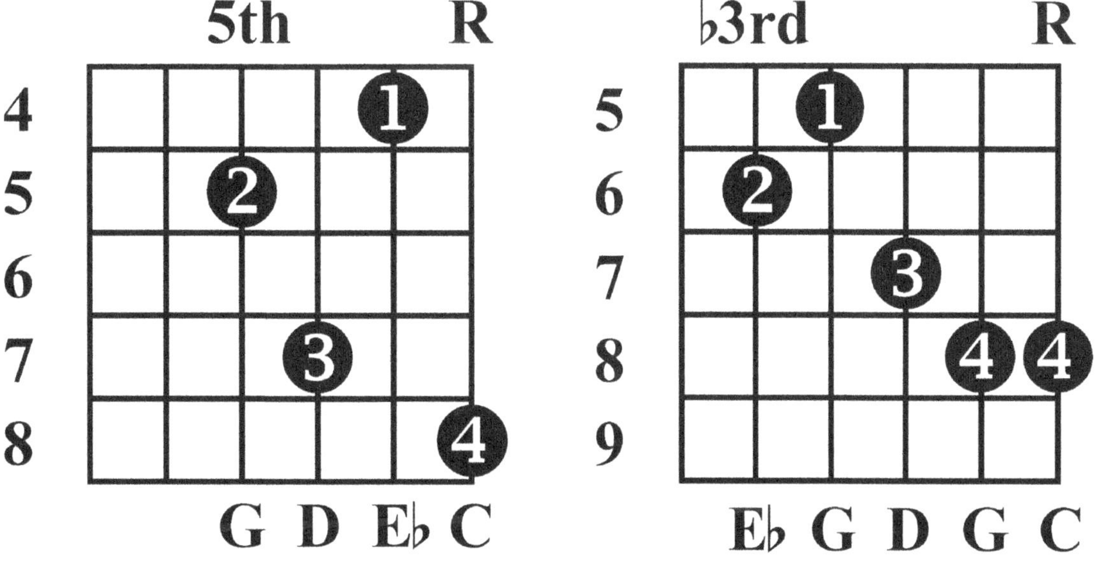

Gm add9

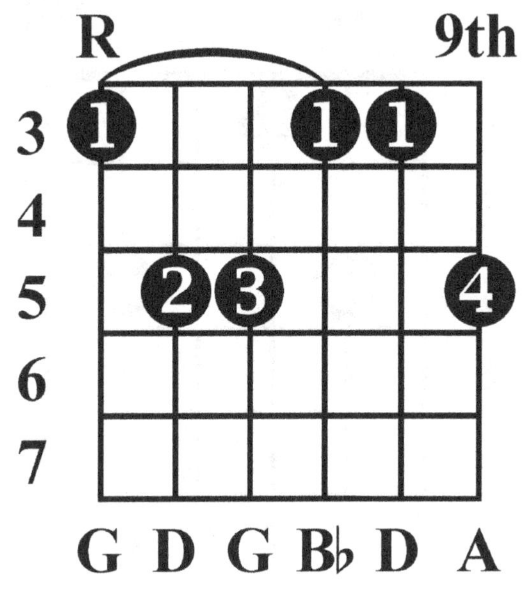

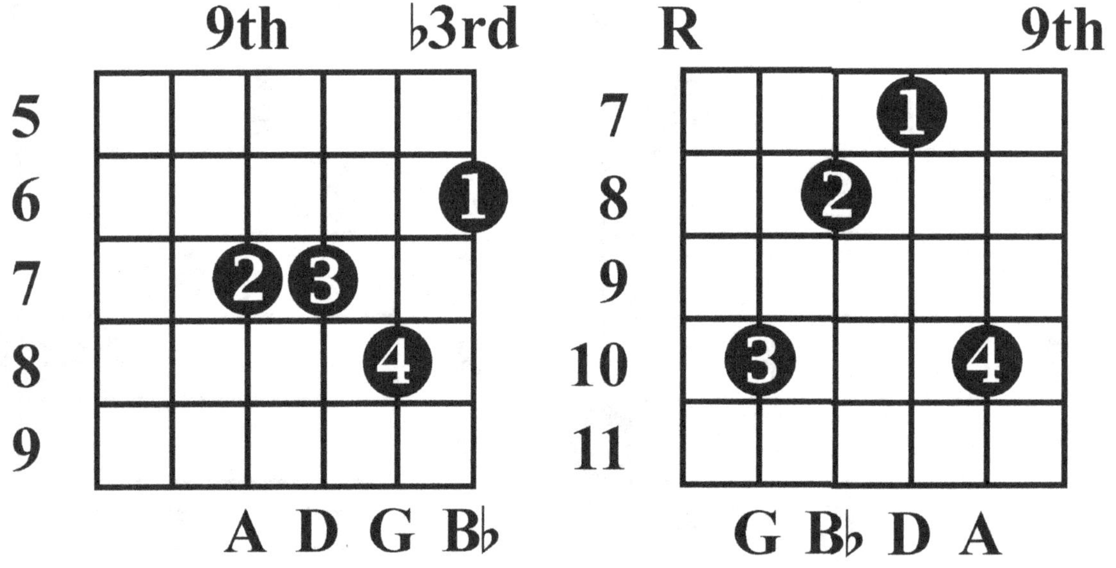

Dm add9

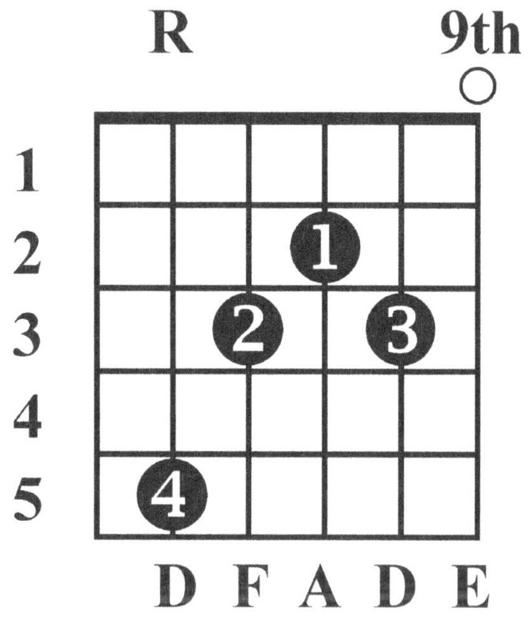

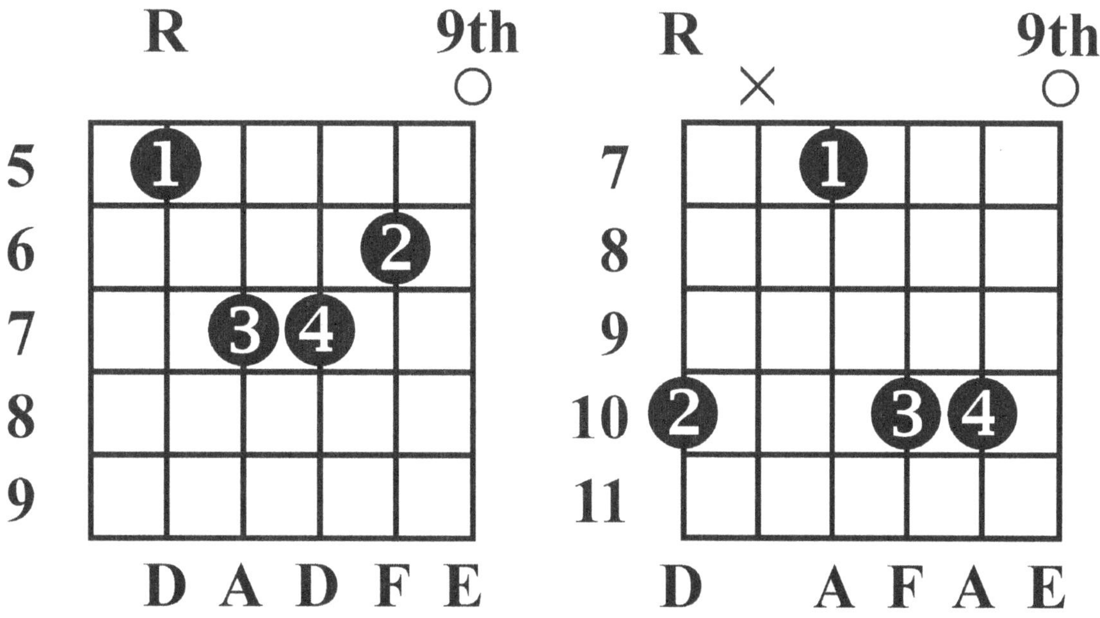

Am add9

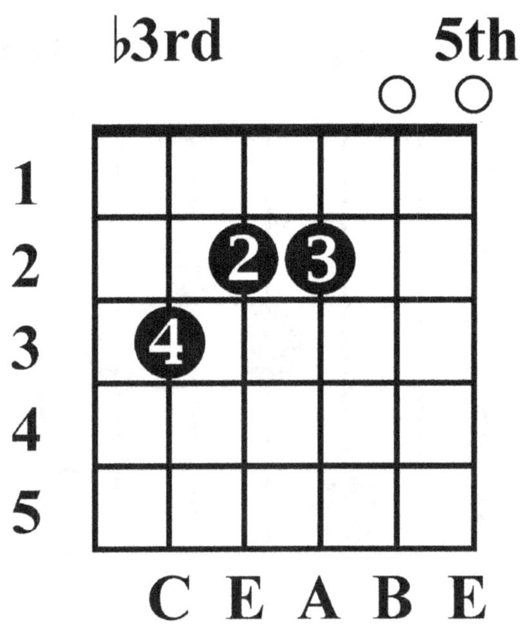

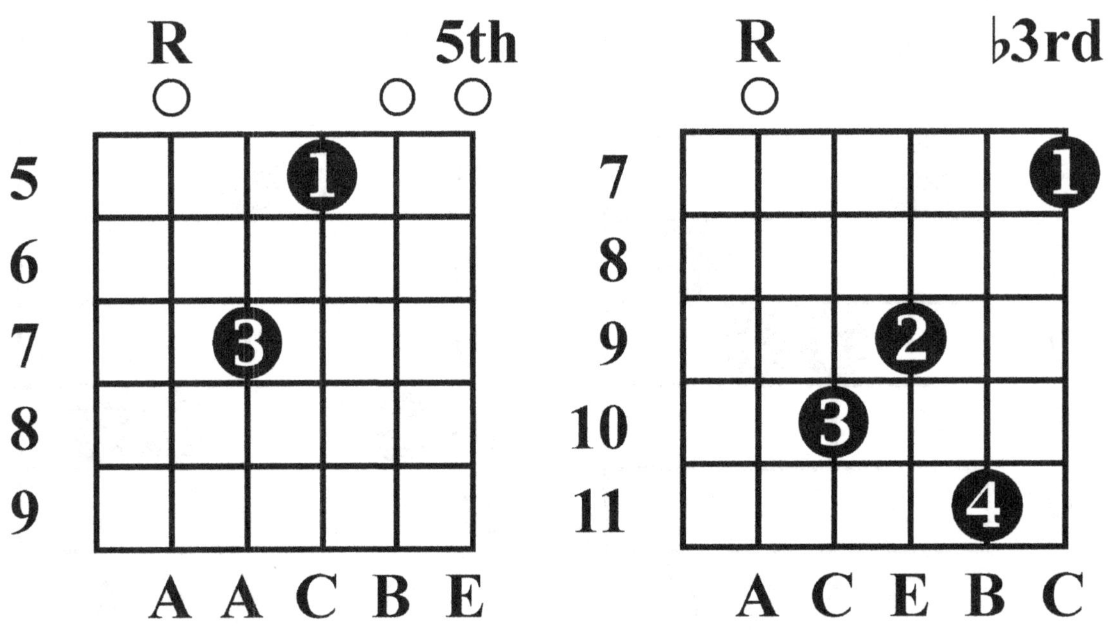

E, B, F, B♭m add9 [69]

Em add9

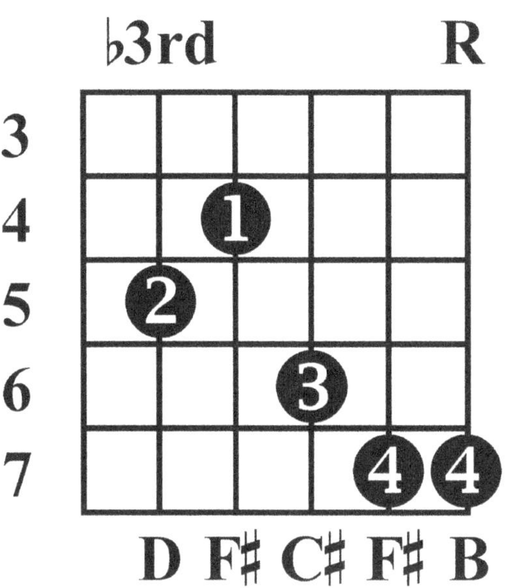

Bm add9

Fm add9

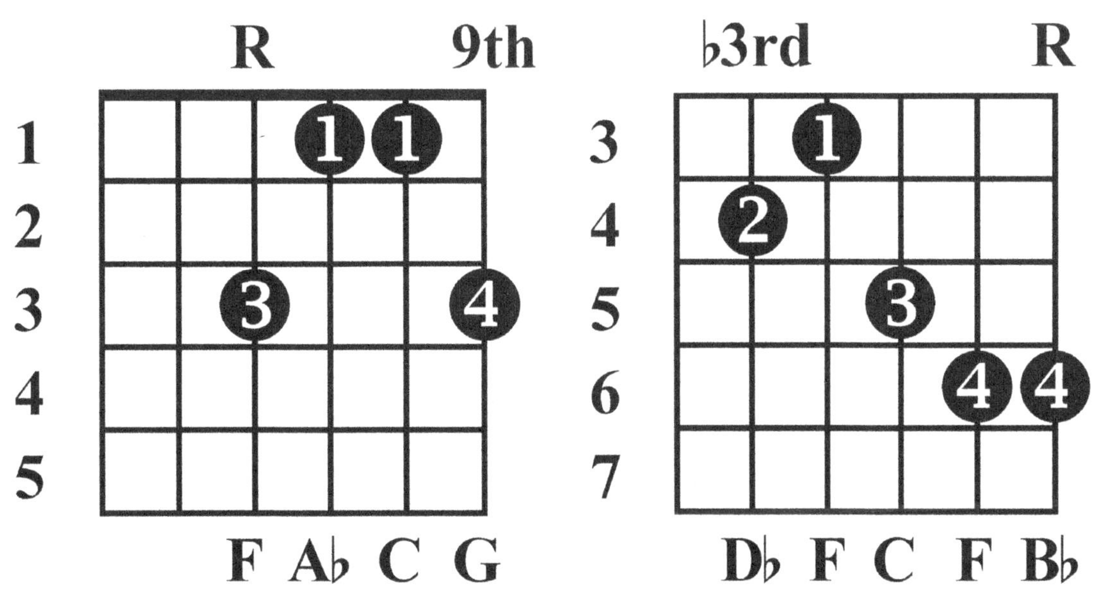

B♭m add9

E♭m, A♭m, D♭m, G♭m / F♯m add9

E♭m add9

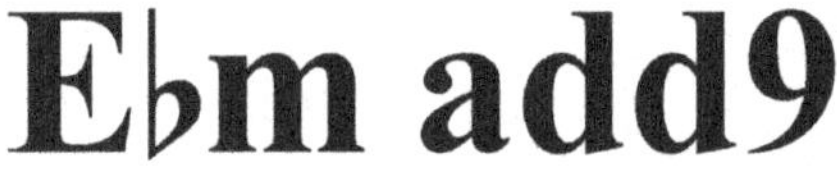

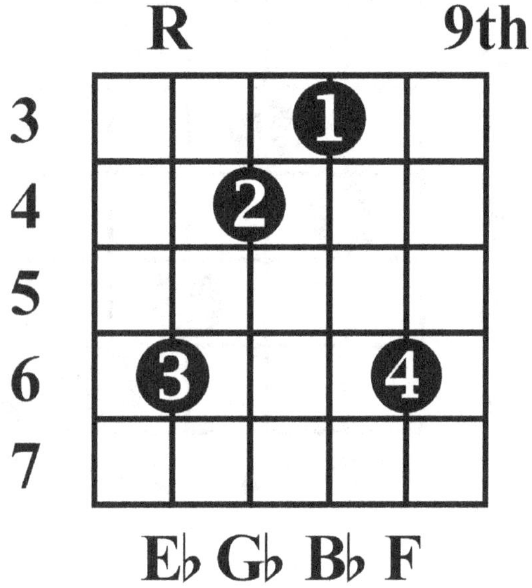
R
9th
3
4
5
6
7
1
2
3
4
E♭ G♭ B♭ F

D♭m add9

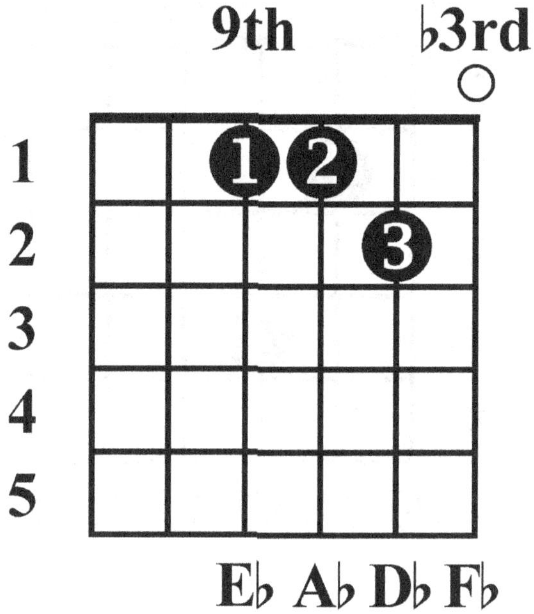
9th
♭3rd
1
2
3
4
5
1
2
3
E♭ A♭ D♭ F♭

A♭m add9

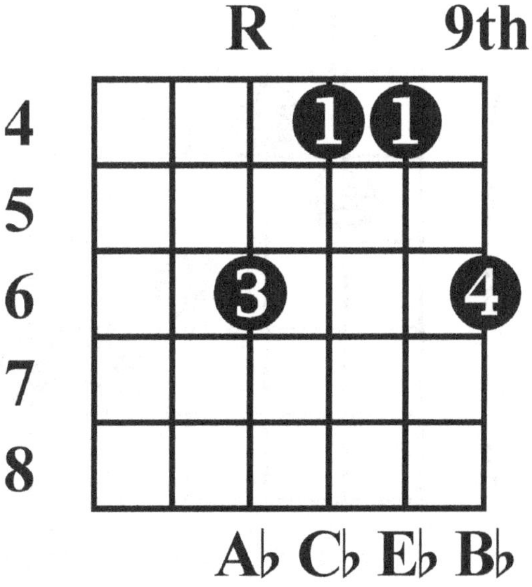
R
9th
4
5
6
7
8
1
1
3
4
A♭ C♭ E♭ B♭

G♭m add9
F♯m add9

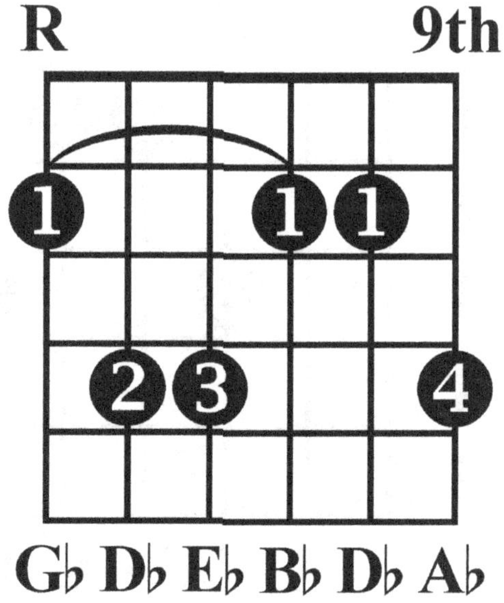
R
9th
1
2
3
4
5
1
1
1
2
3
4
G♭ D♭ E♭ B♭ D♭ A♭

C suspended

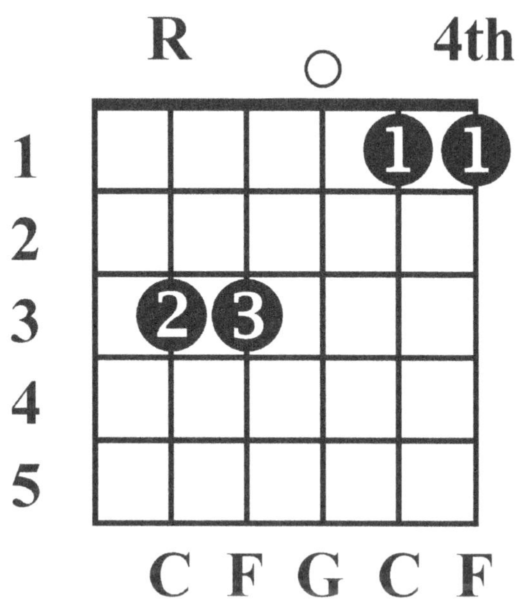

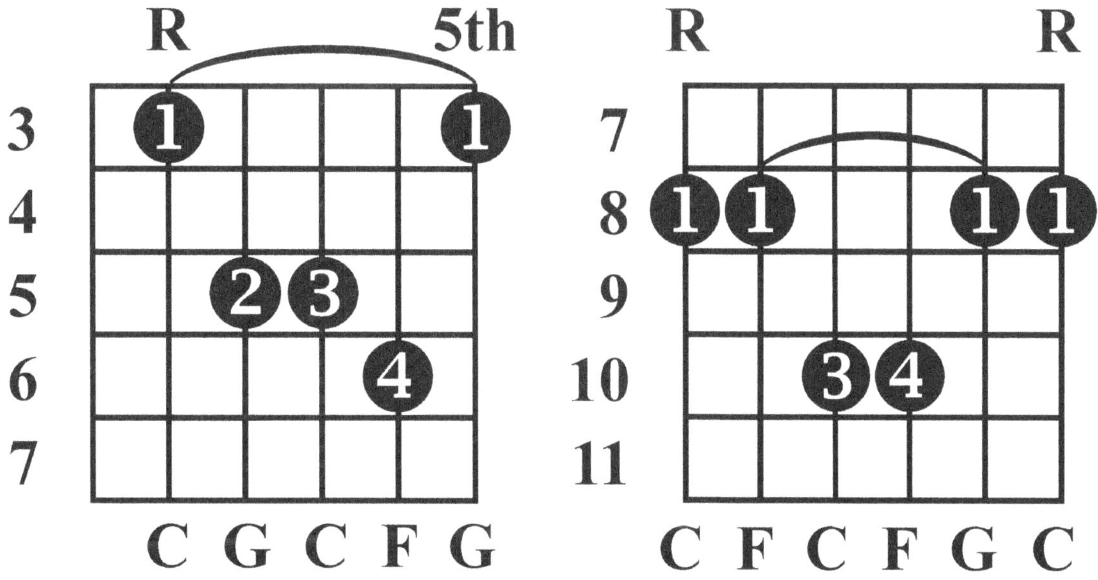

G suspended

R   5th
1
2
3
4
5
G C D C D G

R   R
3
4
5
6
7
G C G C D G

R   4th
5
6
7
8
9
G D G C

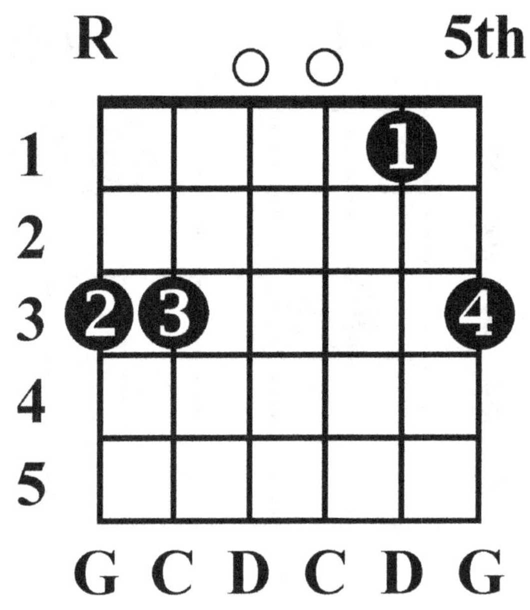

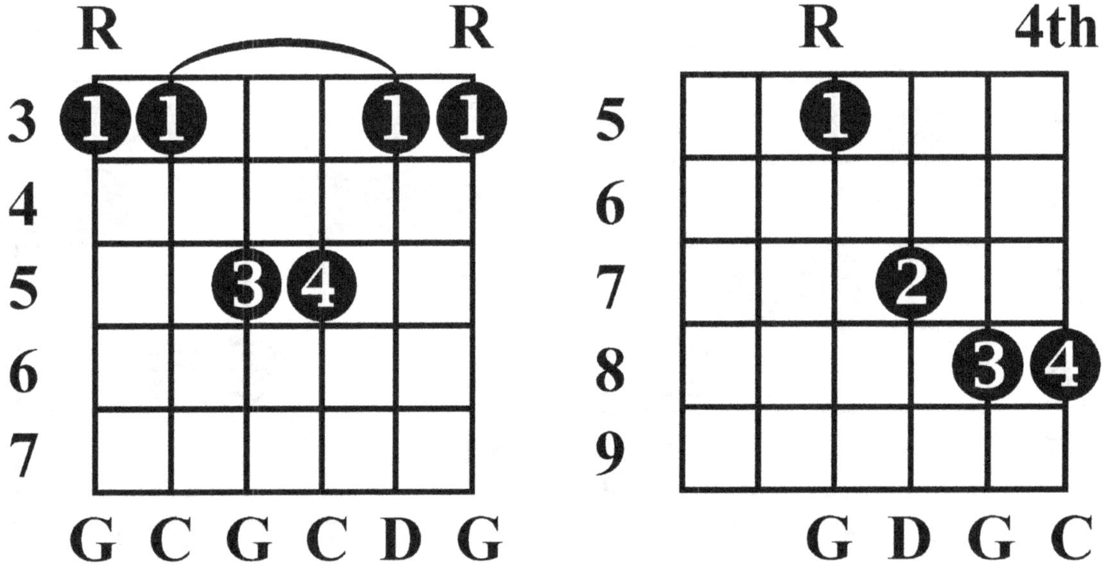

D suspended

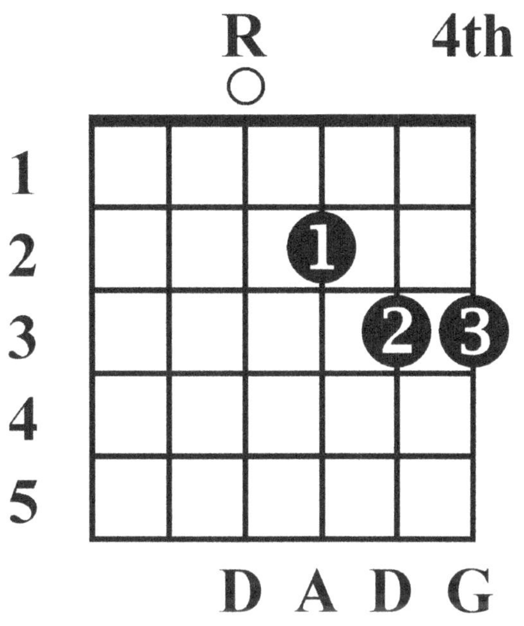

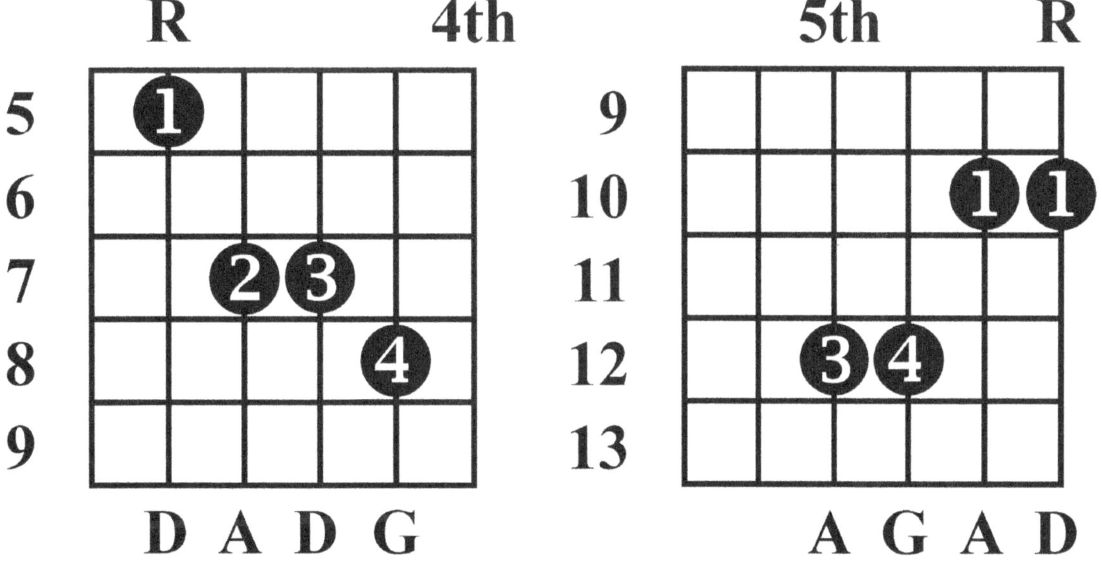

A suspended

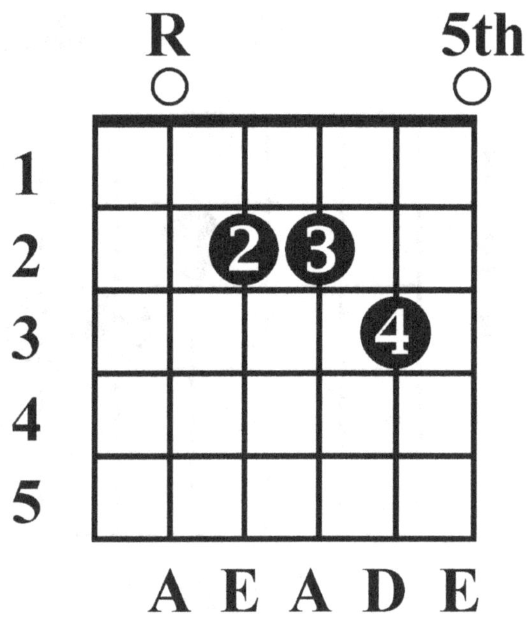

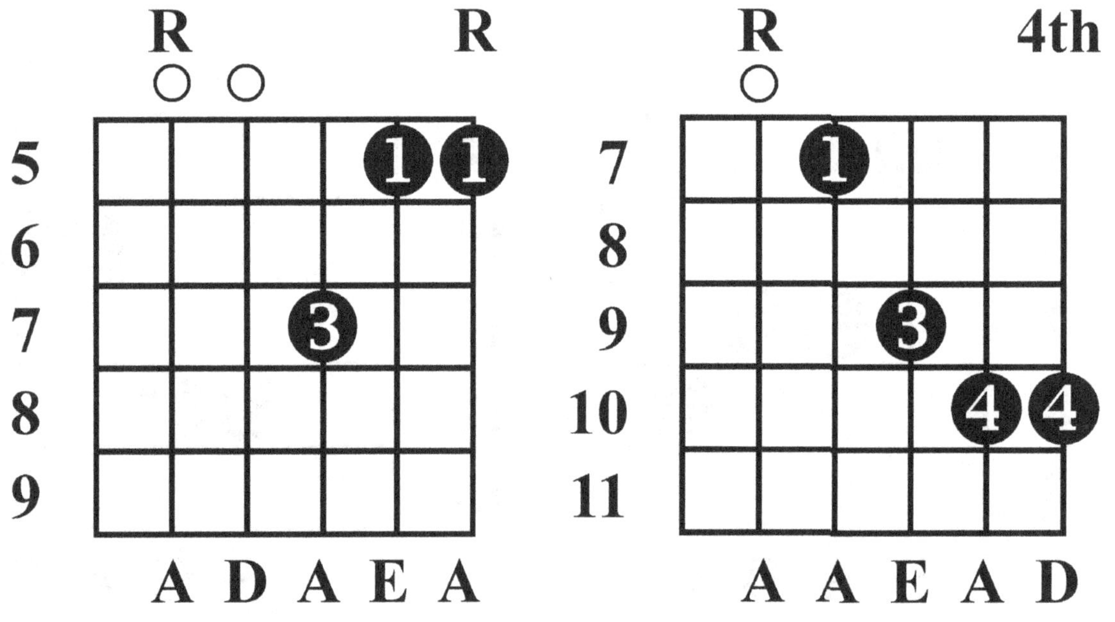

E, B, F, B♭ sus

Esus
R
R
1
2 3 4
3
4
5
E B E A B E

Bsus
R
5th
1
1
3
2 3
4
B F# B E F#

Fsus
R
R
1 1 1
2 3 4
5
F C F B♭ C F

B♭sus
R
5th
1
1
2 3
4
B♭ F B♭ E♭ F

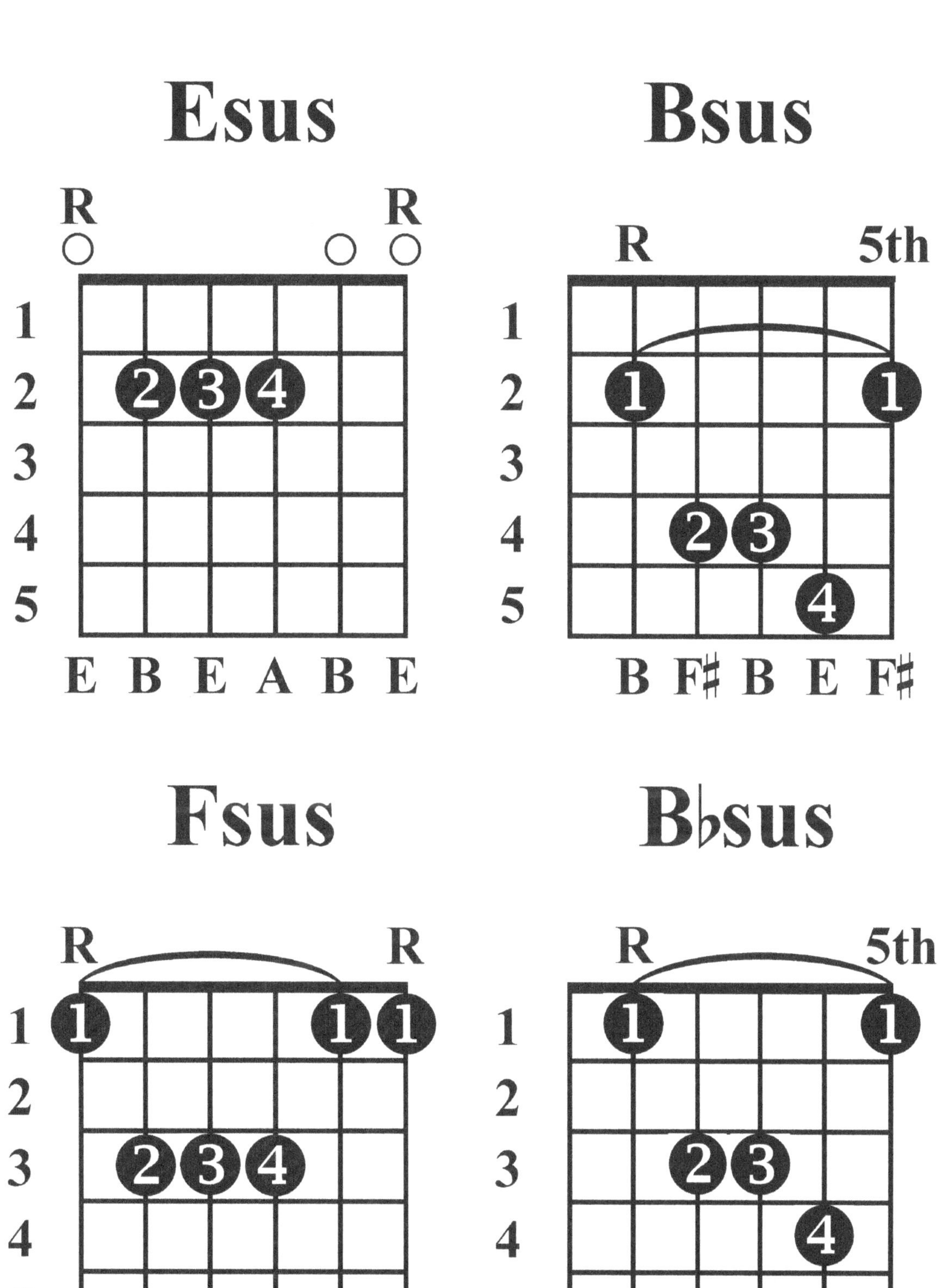

E♭, A♭, D♭, G♭/F♯sus

E♭sus

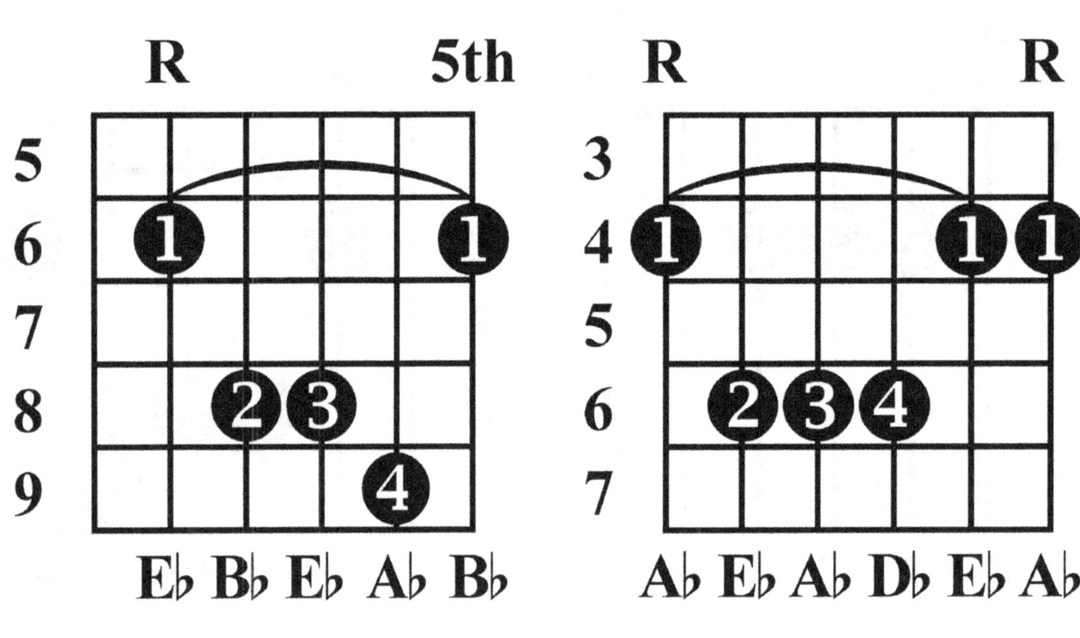

A♭sus

D♭sus

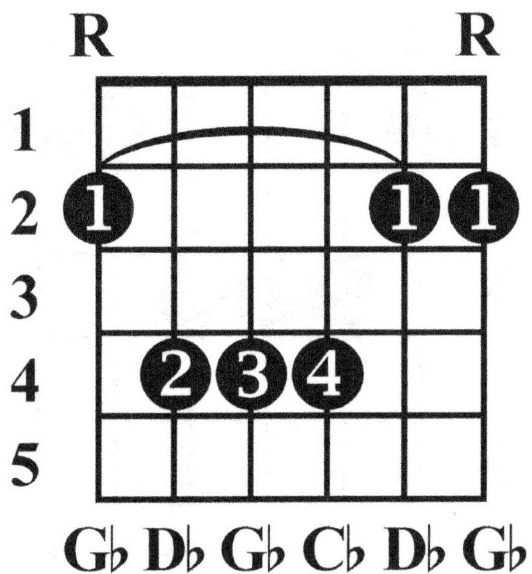

G♭sus
F♯sus

CMaj7add6

R
3rd
1
2
3
4
5
C E A B E

R
6th
3
4
5
6
7
C G B E A
R
×
M7th
7
8
9
10
11
C A E G B

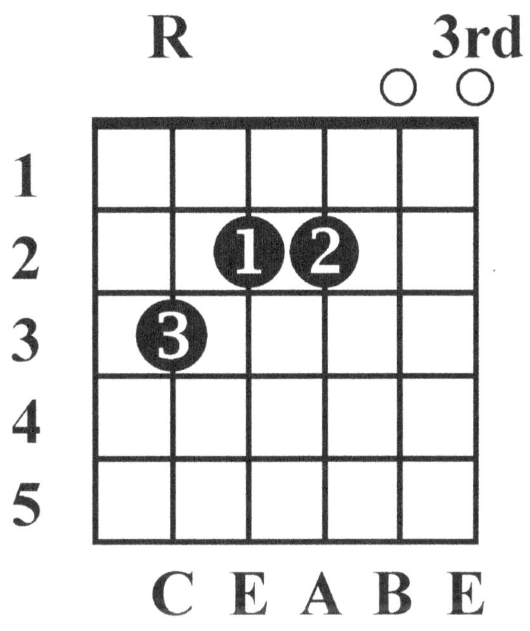

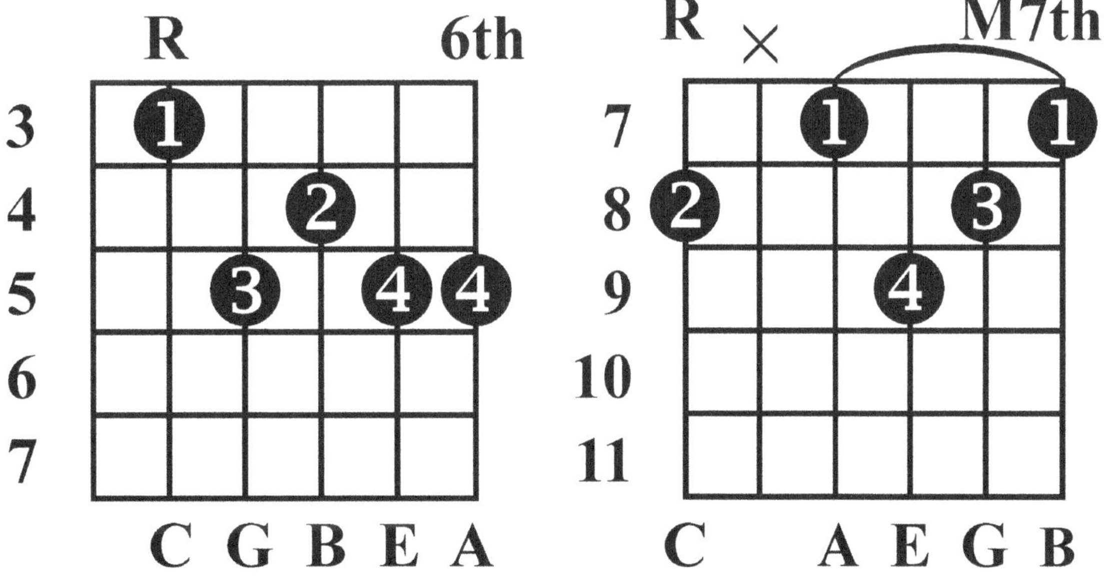

GMaj7add6

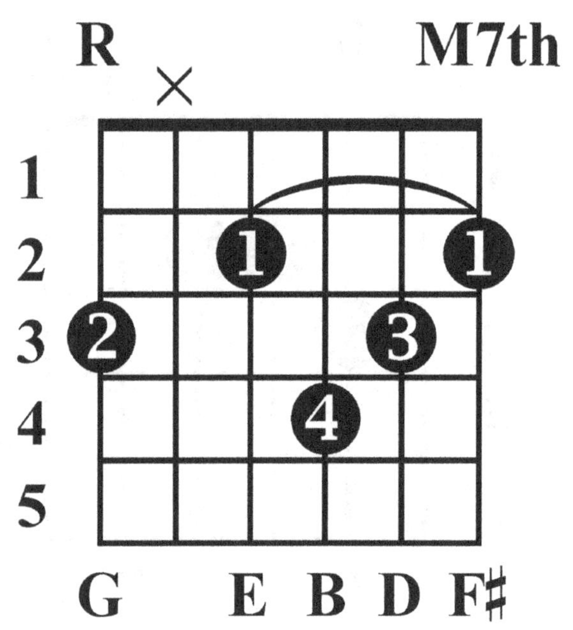

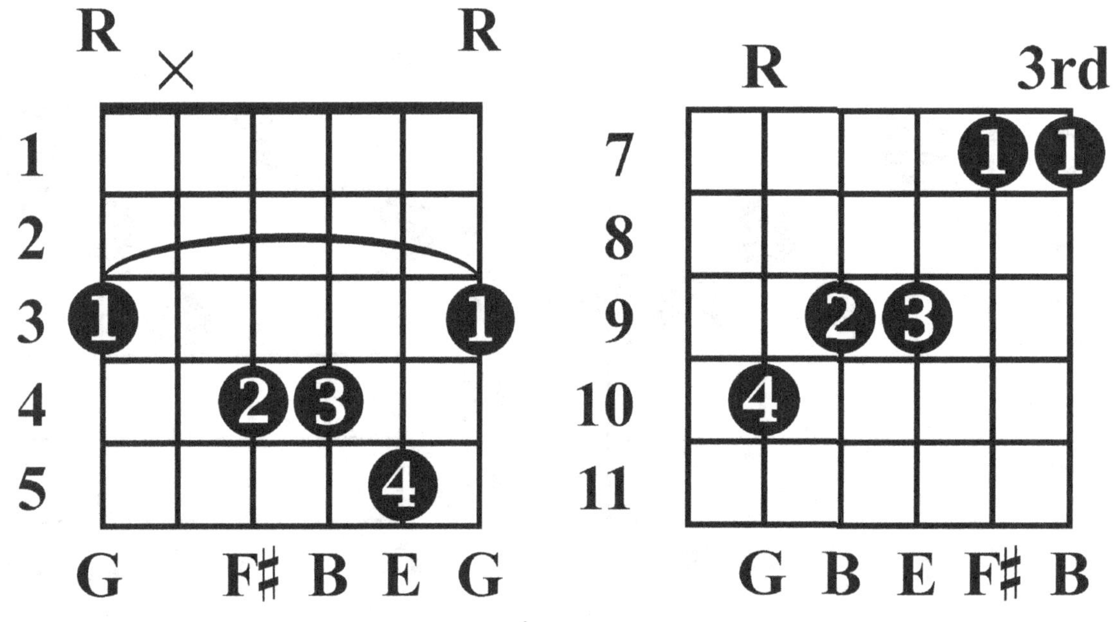

DMaj7add6

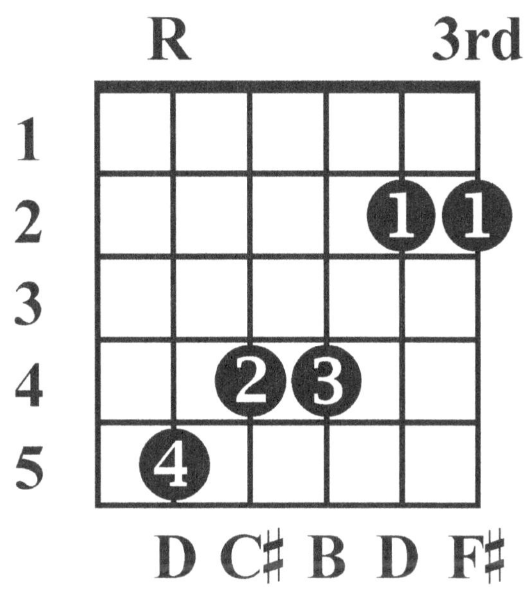

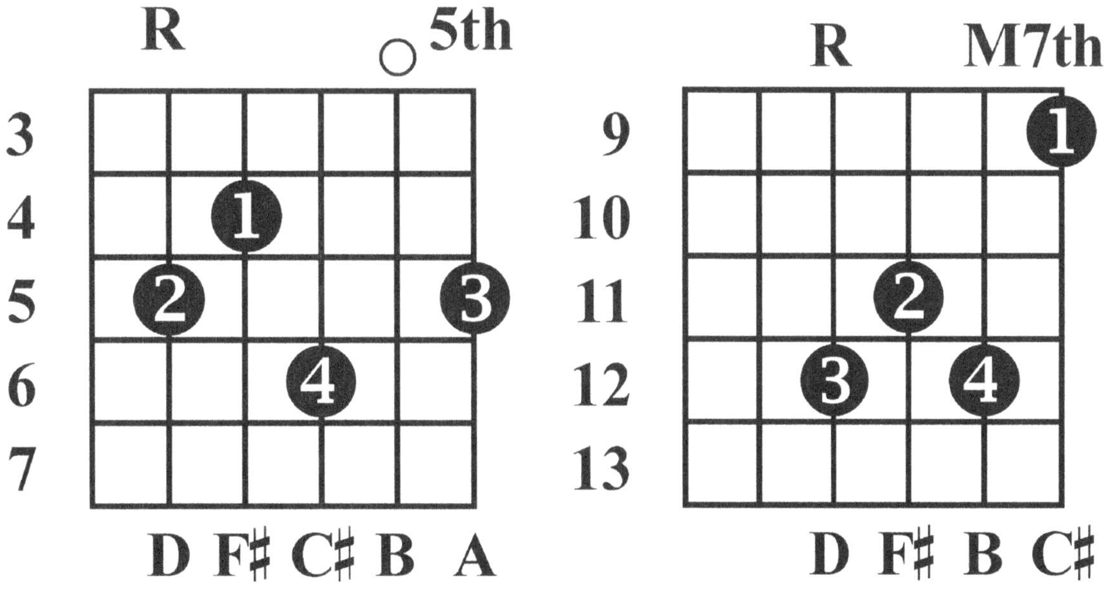

AMaj7add6

R
3rd
1
2
3
4
5
A F# G# C# E

R
M7th
1
2
3
4
5
A F# E C# G#
R
3rd
5
6
7
8
9
A G# E F# C#

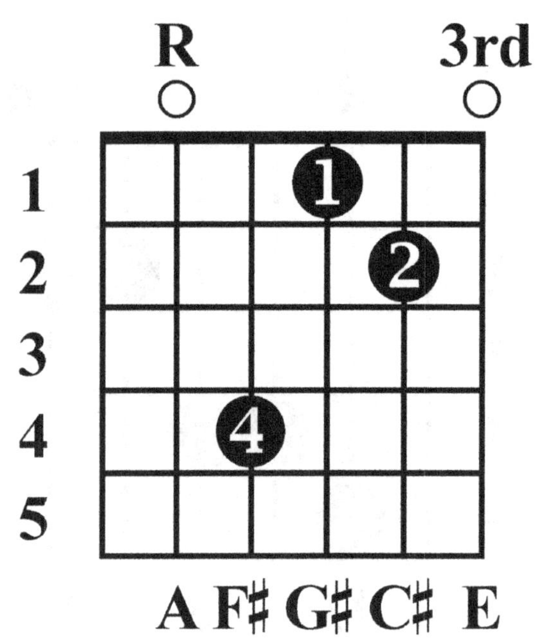

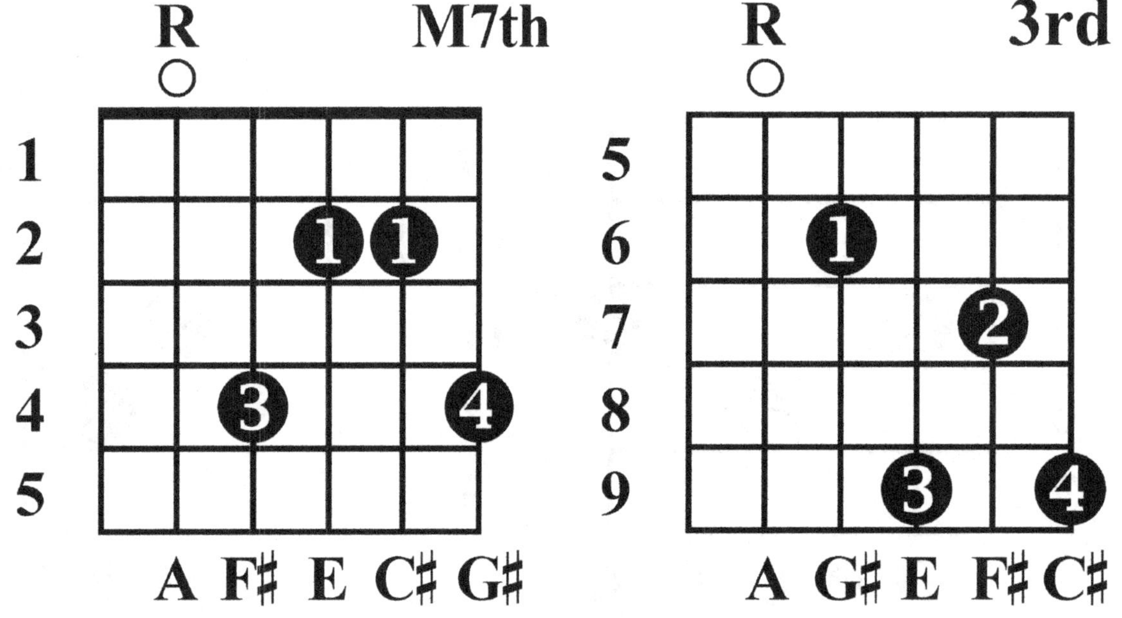

E, B, F, B♭majadd6

Emaj7add6 Bmaj7add6

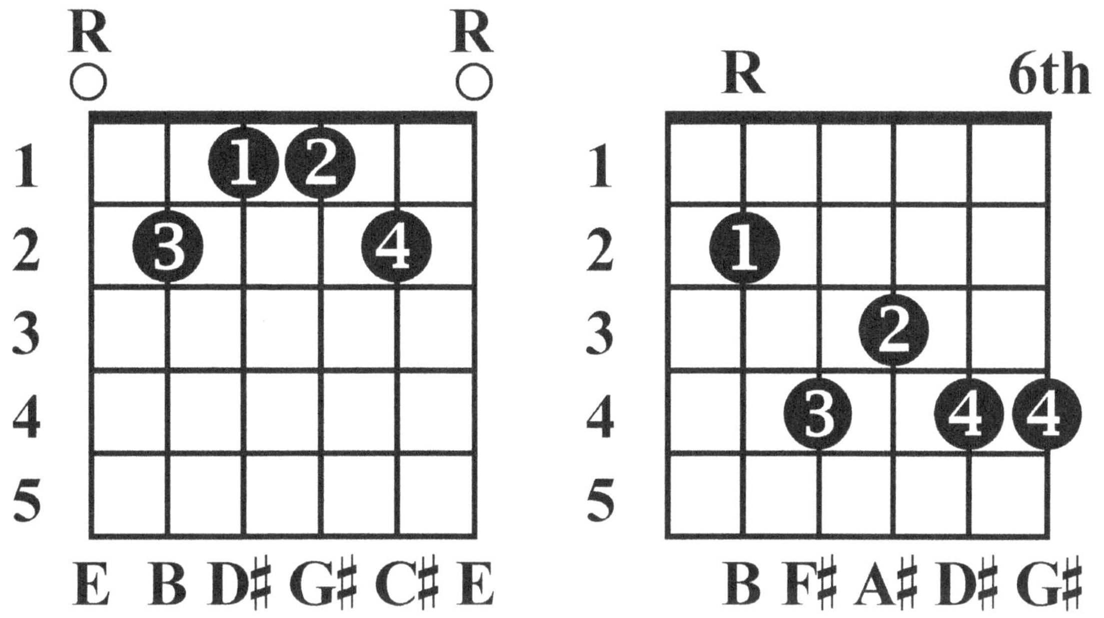

Fmaj7add6 B♭maj7add6

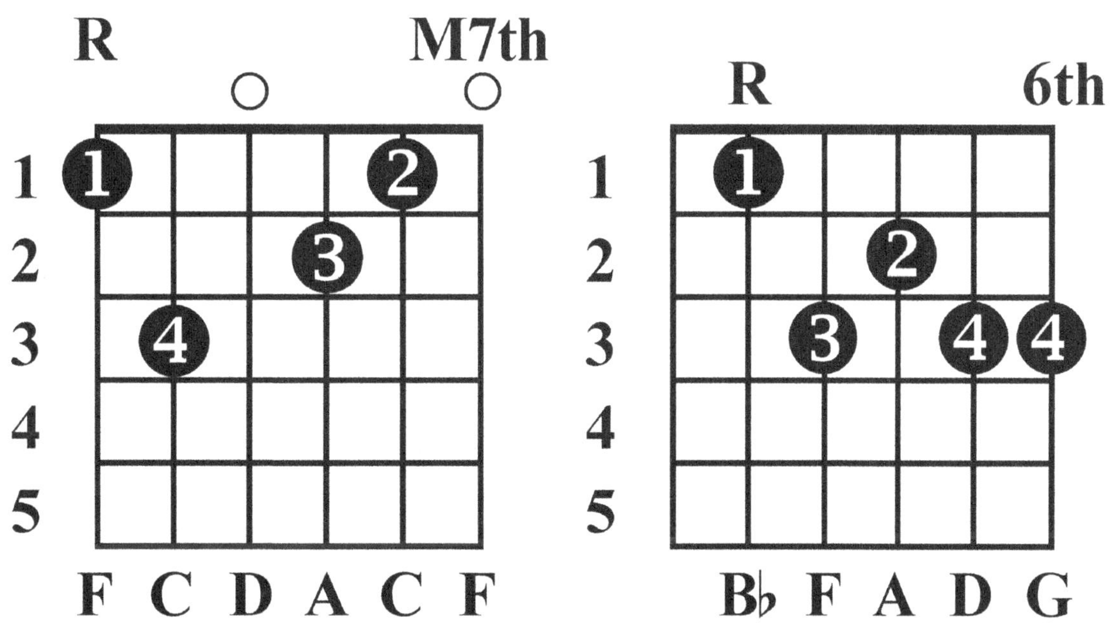

E♭, A♭, D♭, G♭ / F♯maj7add6

E♭maj7add6 A♭maj7add6

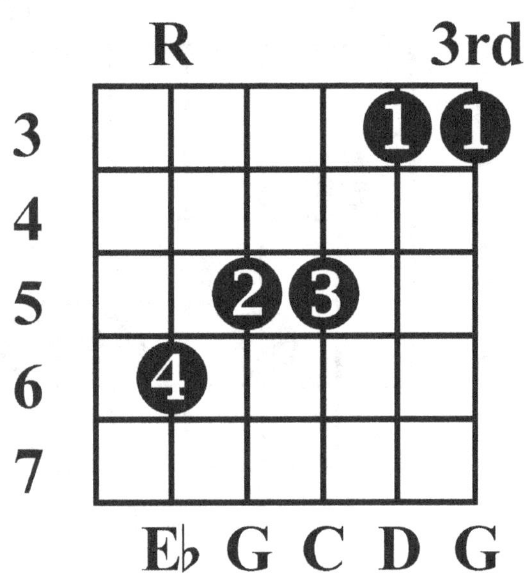

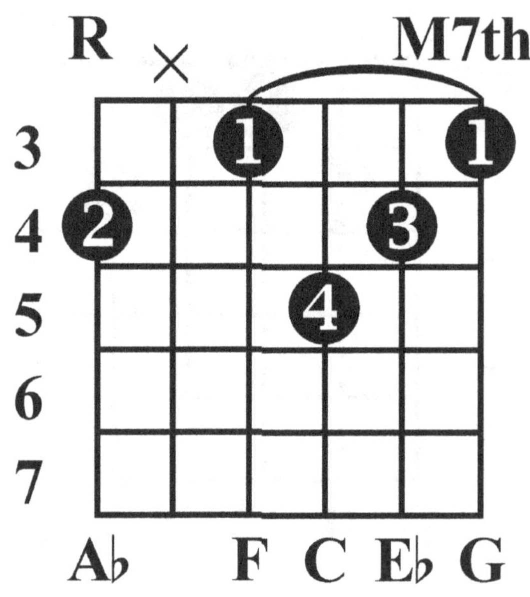

D♭maj7add6

G♭maj7add6
F♯maj7add6

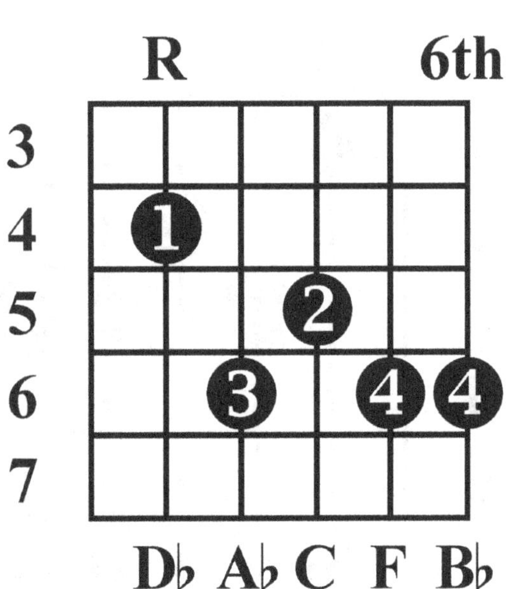

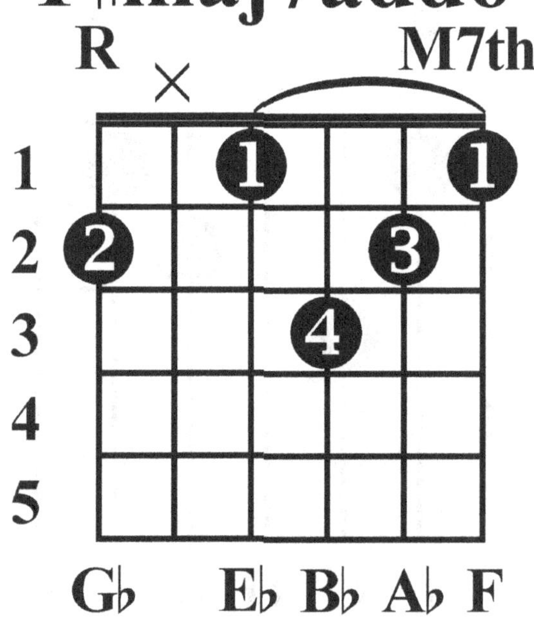

C, G, D, Amaj9

Cmaj9
R
3rd
1
2
3
4
5
C E B D E
Gmaj9
R
M7th
1
2
3
4
5
G B D A B F#

Dmaj9
R
3rd
3
4
5
6
7
D E A C# F#
Amaj9
R
5th
3
4
5
6
7
A G# C# B E

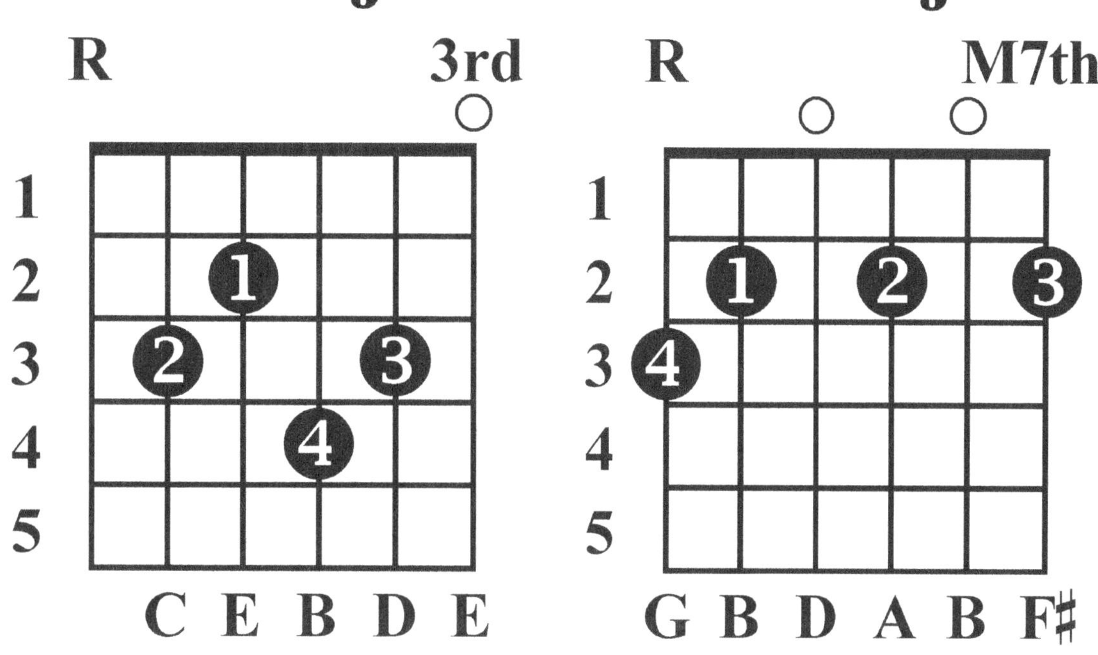

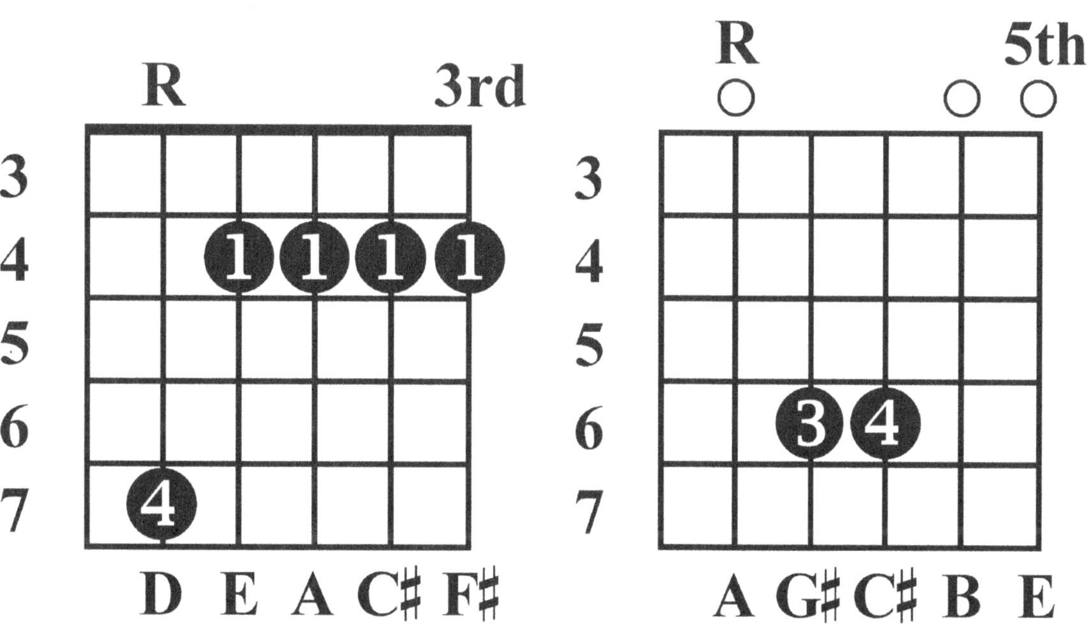

E, B, F, B♭maj9

Emaj9

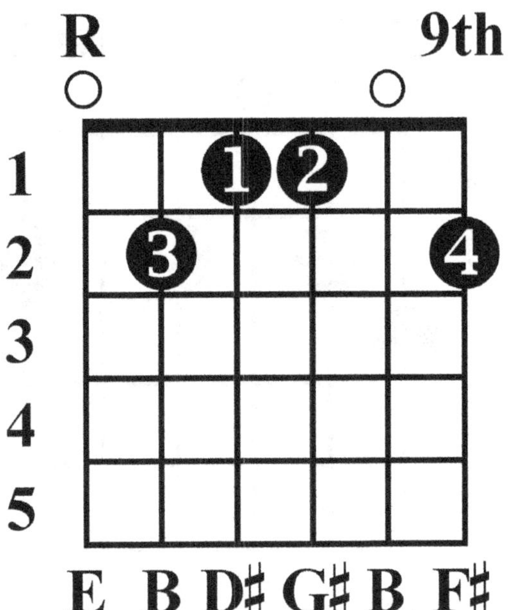

Bmaj9

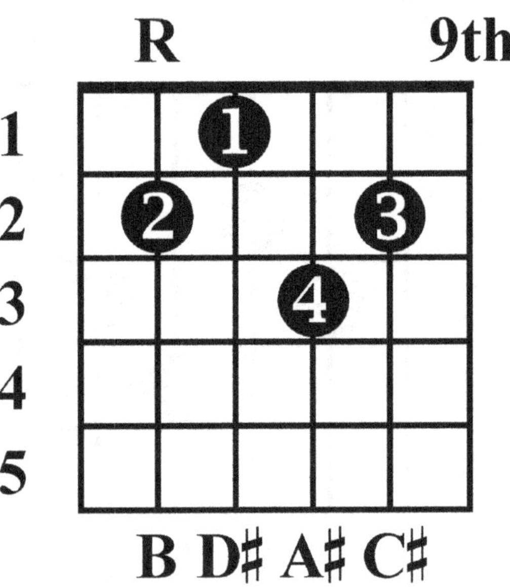

Fmaj9

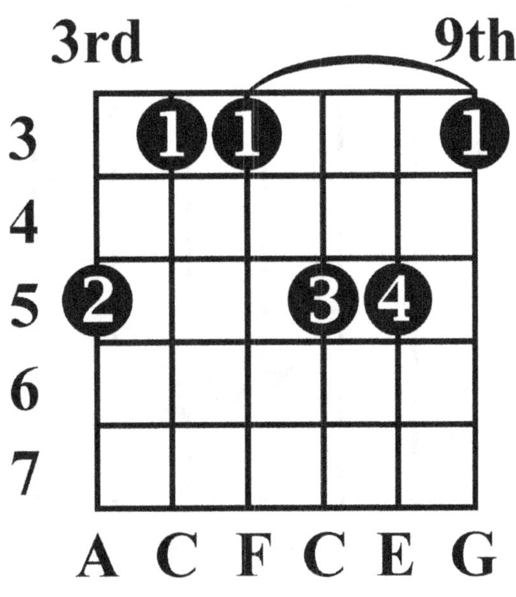

B♭maj9

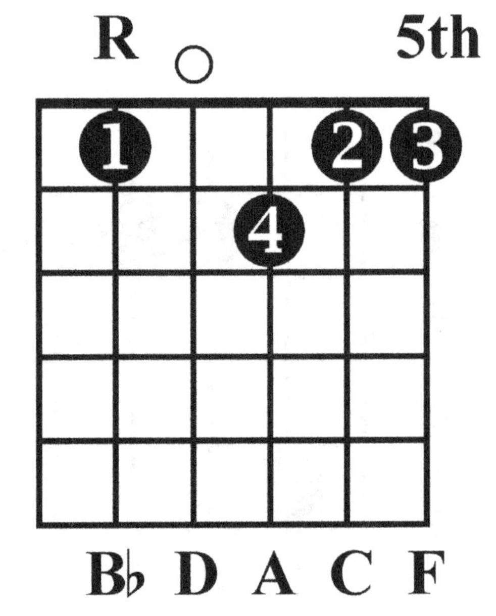

E♭, A♭, D♭, G♭/F#maj9

E♭maj9

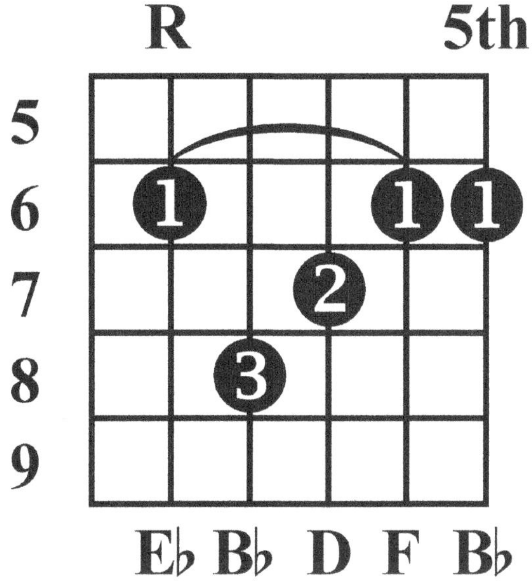

A♭maj9

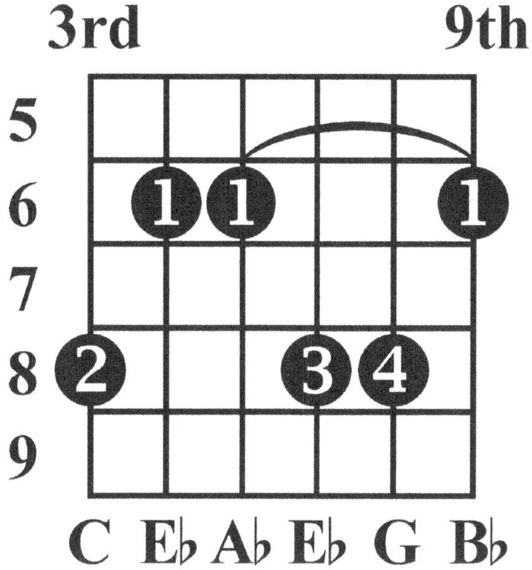

D♭maj9

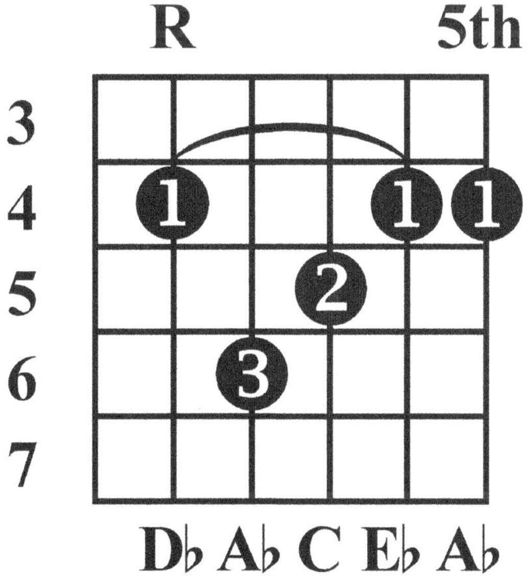

G♭maj9
F#maj9

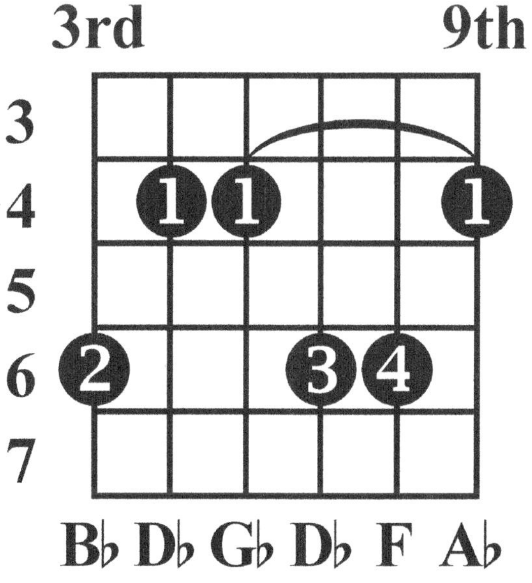

C, G, D, Amaj13

Cmaj13

Gmaj13

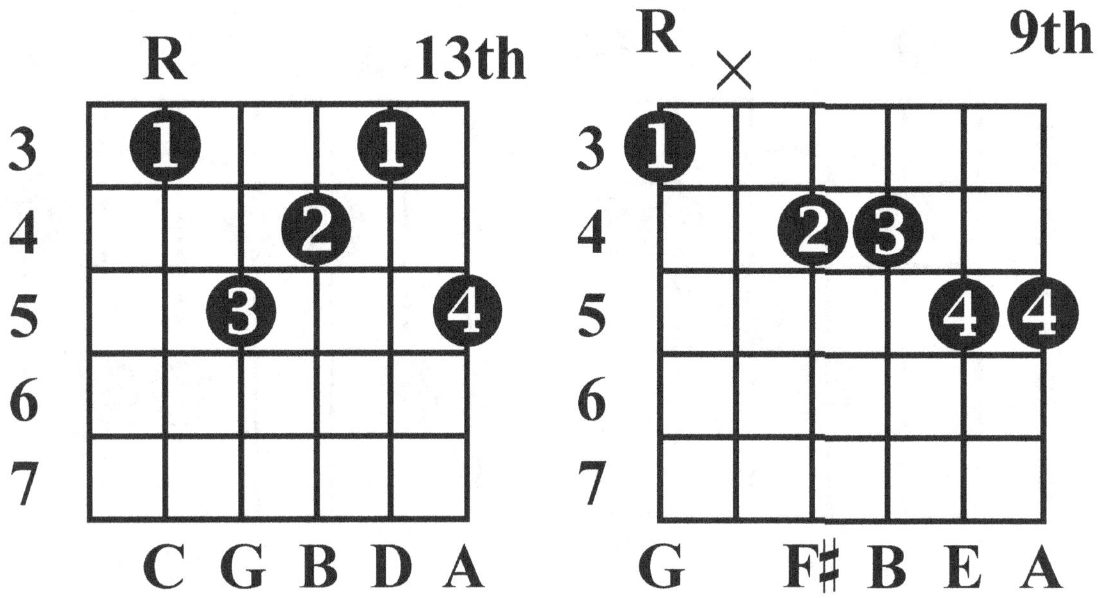

Dmaj13

Amaj13

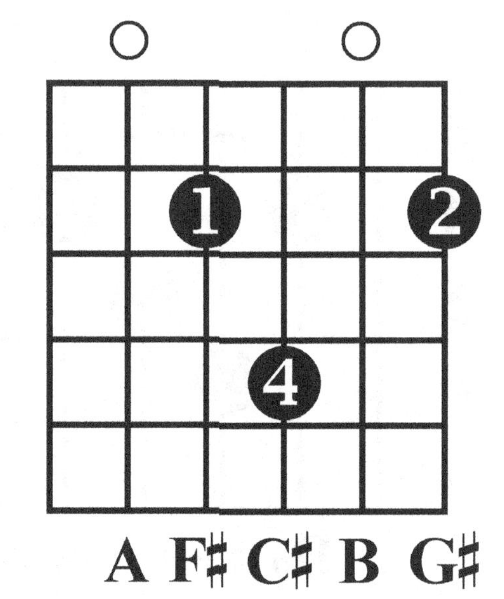

E, B, F, B♭maj13 ⁸⁷

Emaj13

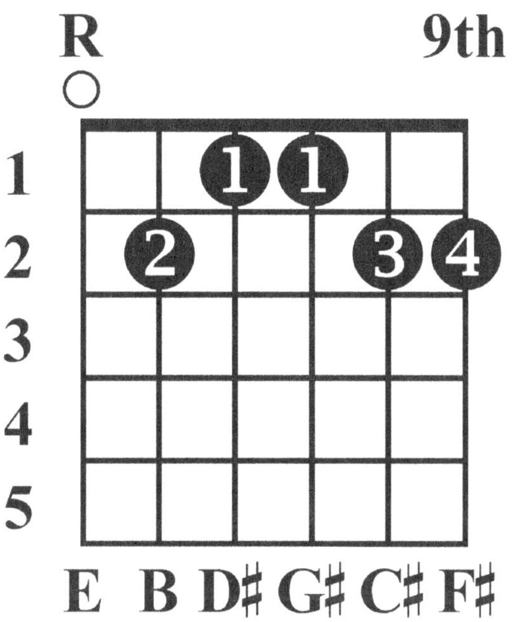

Bmaj13

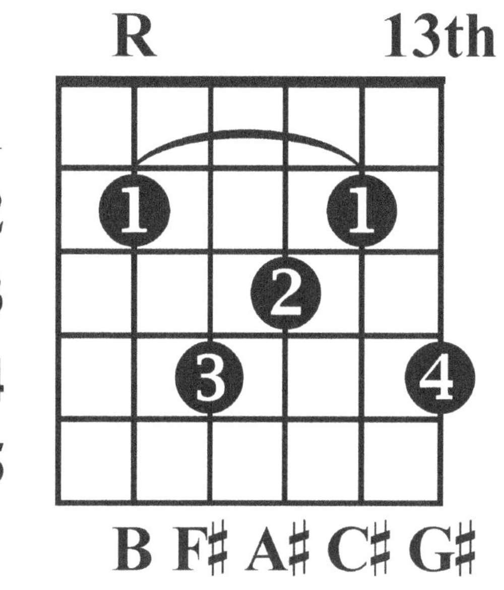

Fmaj13

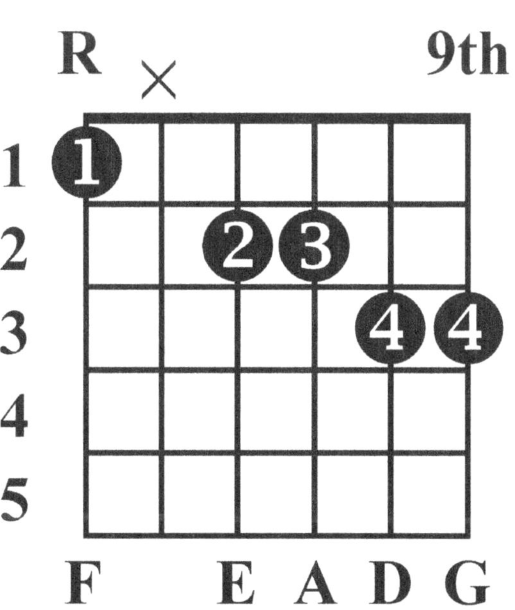

B♭maj13

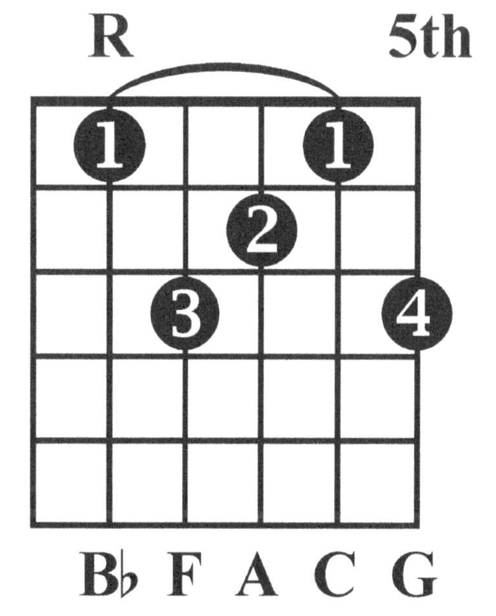

E♭, A♭, D♭, G♭/F♯maj13

E♭maj13

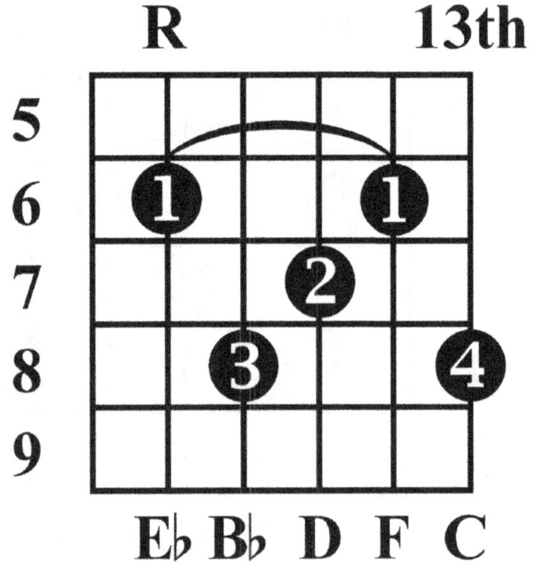

R   13th

5
6 — ① ①
7 — ②
8 — ③ ④
9

E♭ B♭ D F C

A♭maj13

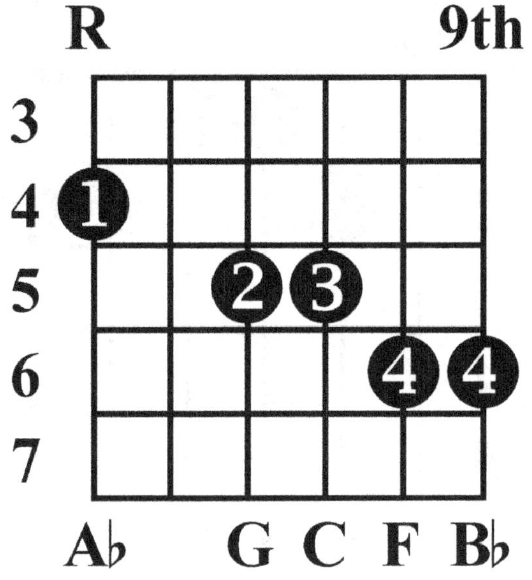

R   9th

3
4 — ①
5 — ② ③
6 — ④ ④
7

A♭ G C F B♭

D♭maj13

R   13th

3
4 — ① ①
5 — ②
6 — ③ ④
7

D♭ A♭ C E♭ B♭

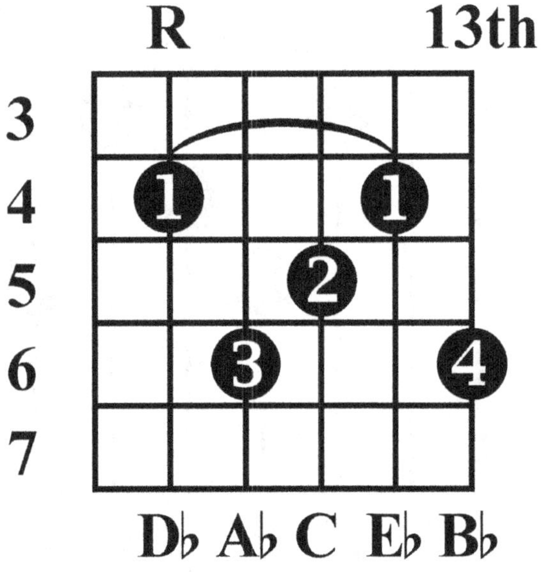

G♭maj13
F♯maj13

R ×   9th

1
2 — ①
3 — ② ③
4 — ④ ④
5

G♭ F B♭ E♭ A♭

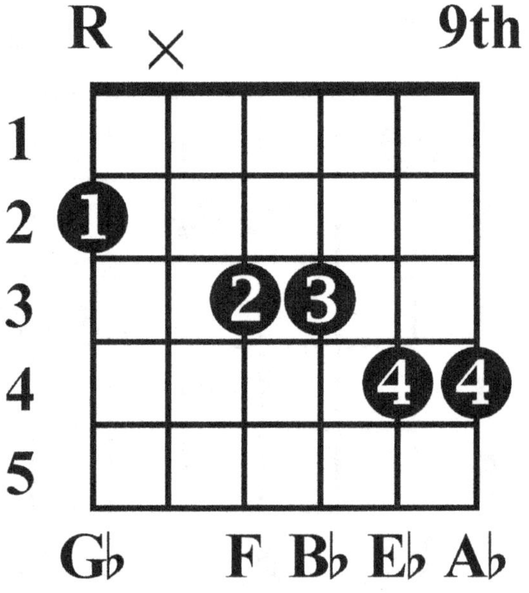

C, G, D, A6/9

C6/9
R
5th
1
2
3
4
5
C E A D G
G6/9
R
6th
1
2
3
4
5
G B D A B E
D6/9
R
9th
1
2
3
4
5
D F# A B E
A6/9
R
5th
3
4
5
6
7
A F# C# B E

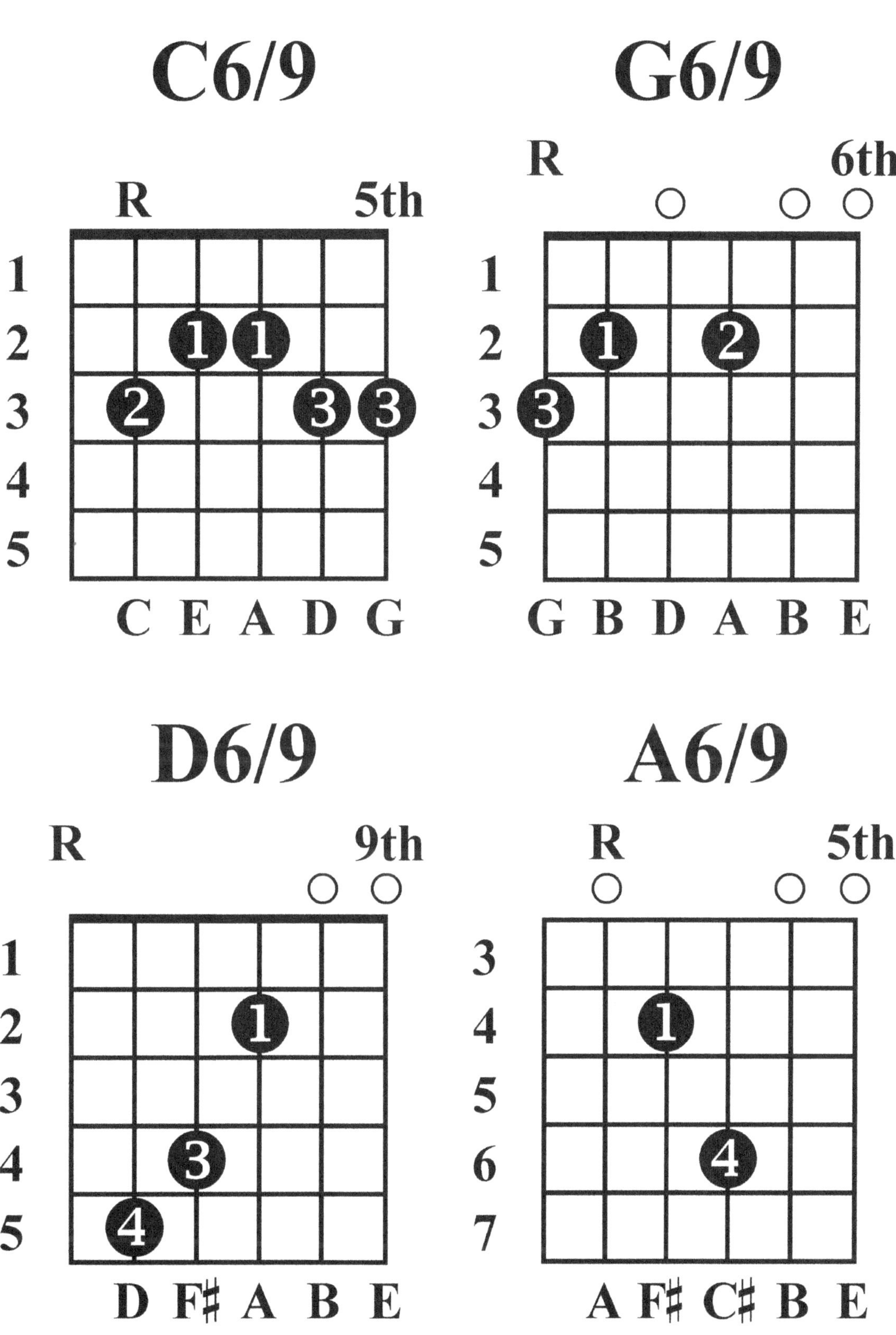

E, B, F, B♭6/9

E6/9

B6/9

F6/9

B♭6/9

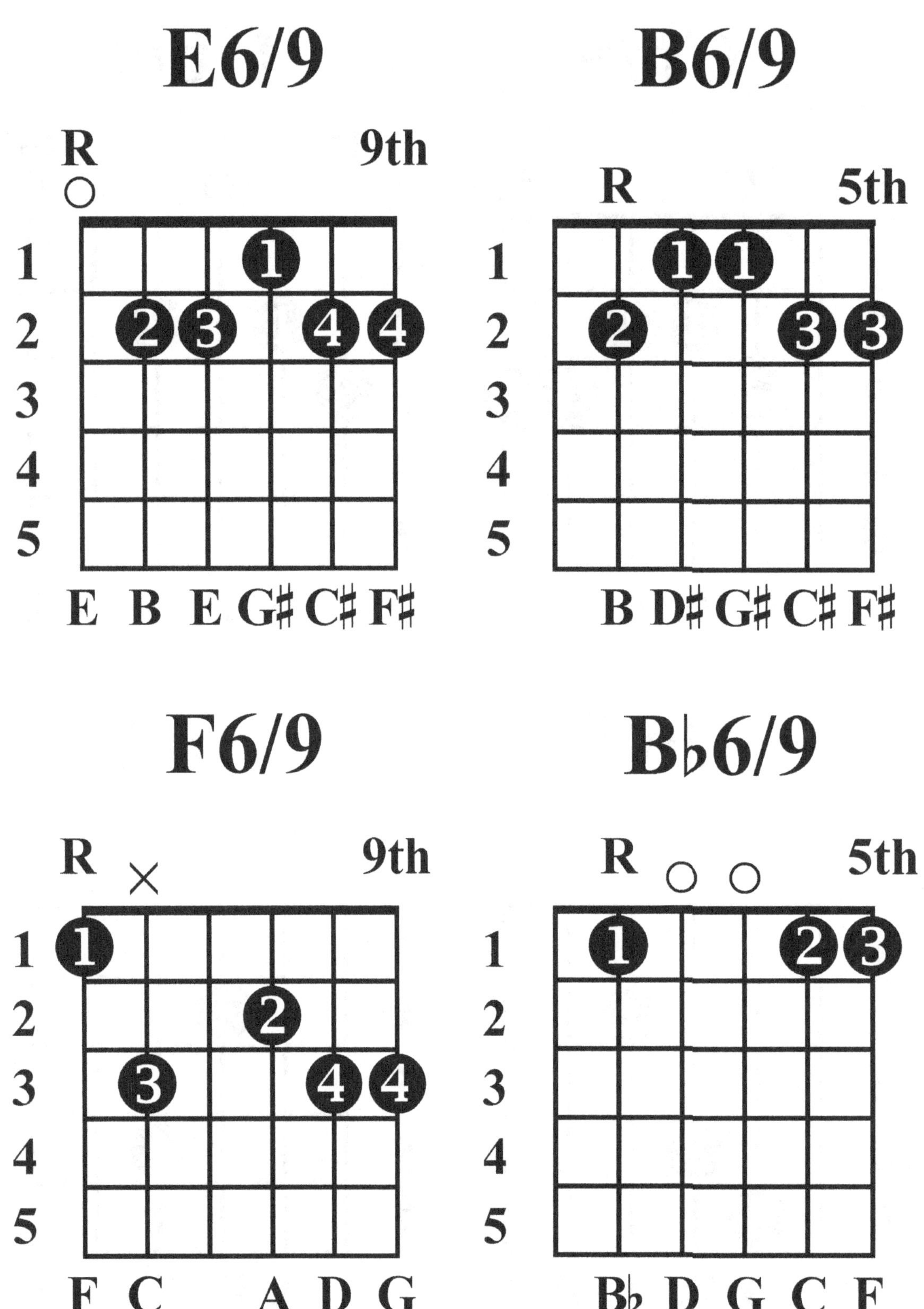

Eb, Ab, Db, Gb/F#6/9

Eb 6/9

Ab 6/9

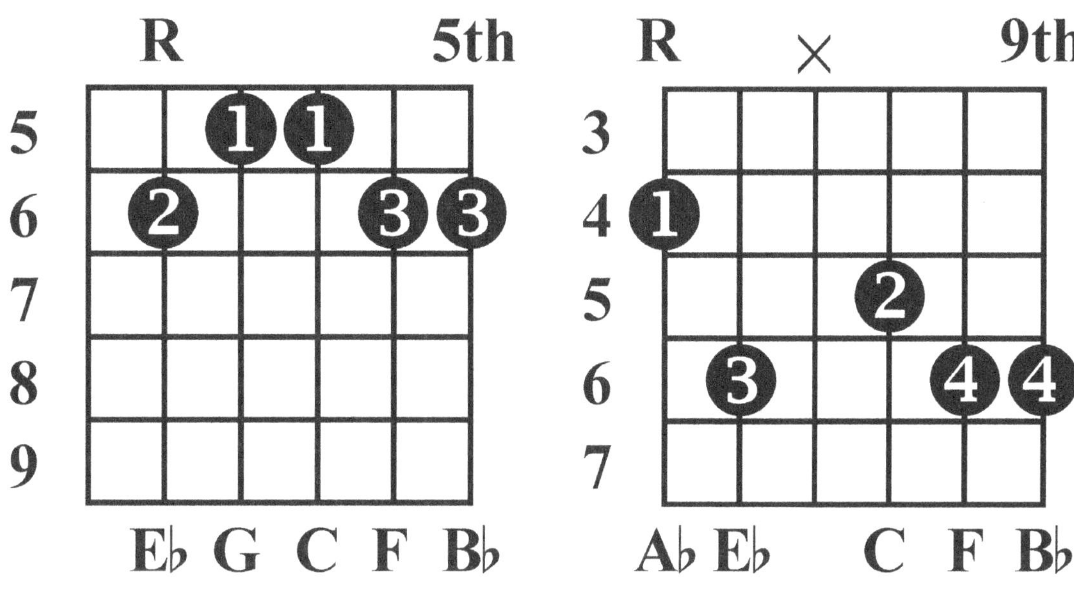

Db 6/9

Gb 6/9, F#6/9

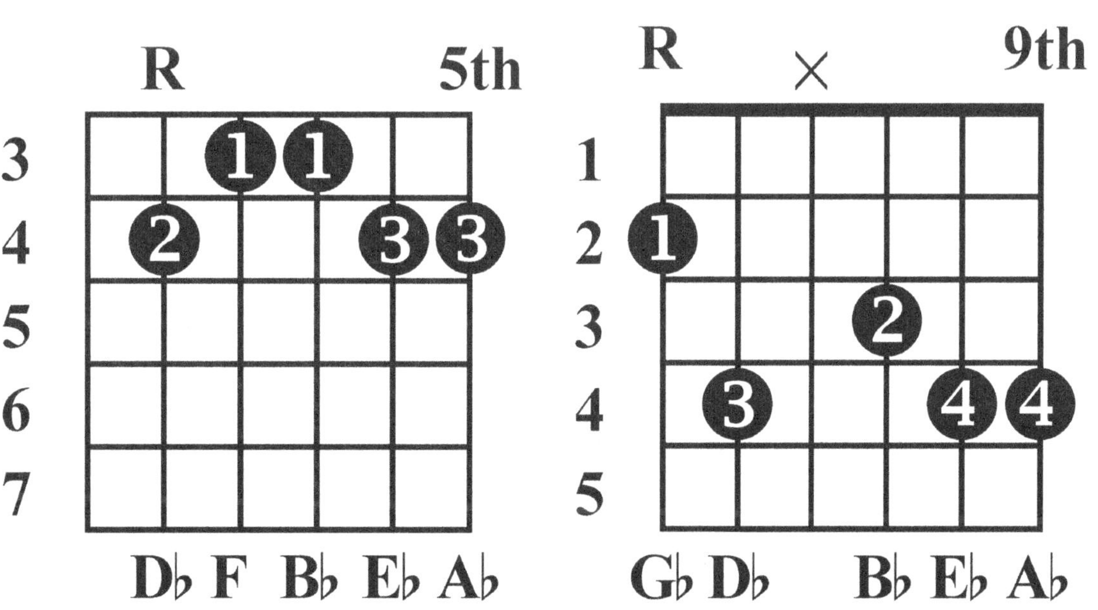

Diminished

F°, A♭°, B°, D°

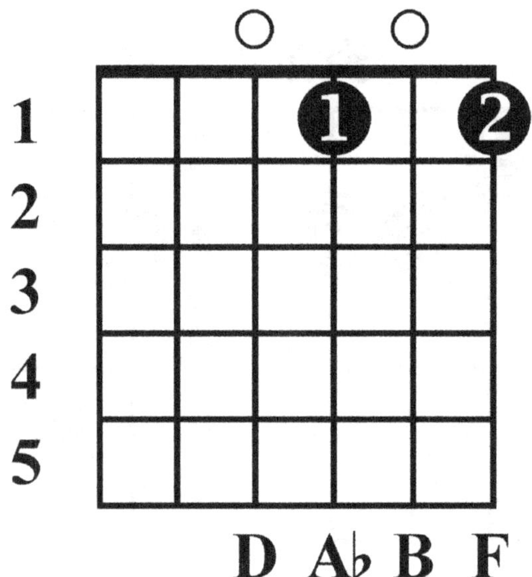

G♭/F♯° A°, C°, E♭°   G°, B♭°, D♭°, E°

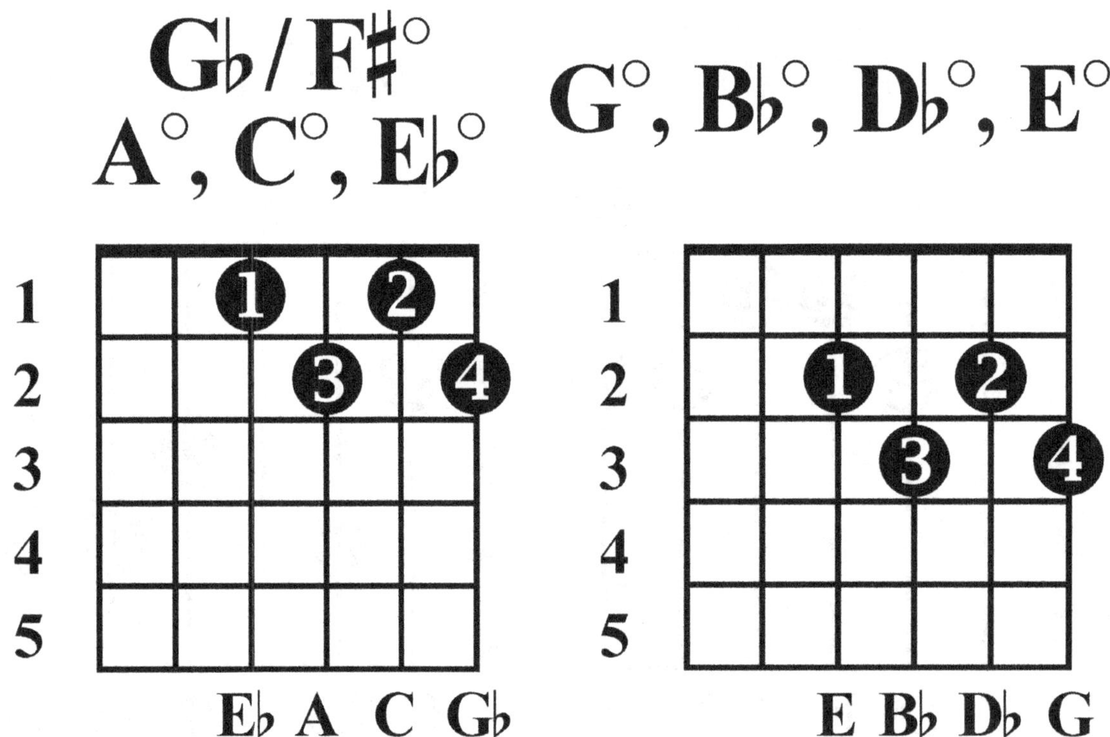

Another Diminished Form

F°, A♭°, B°, D°

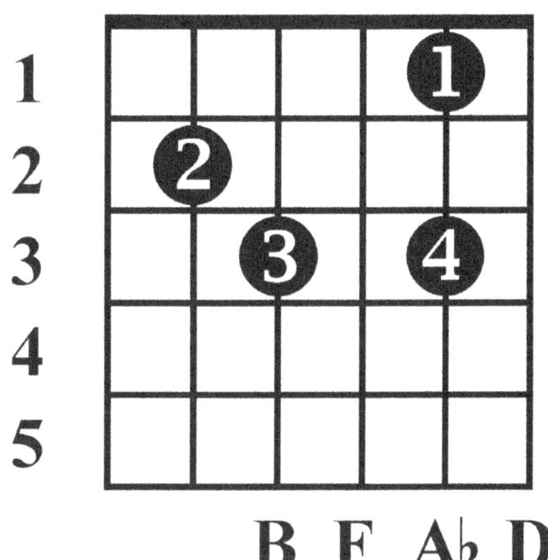

G♭/F#°
A°, C°, E♭°

G°, B♭°, D♭°, E°

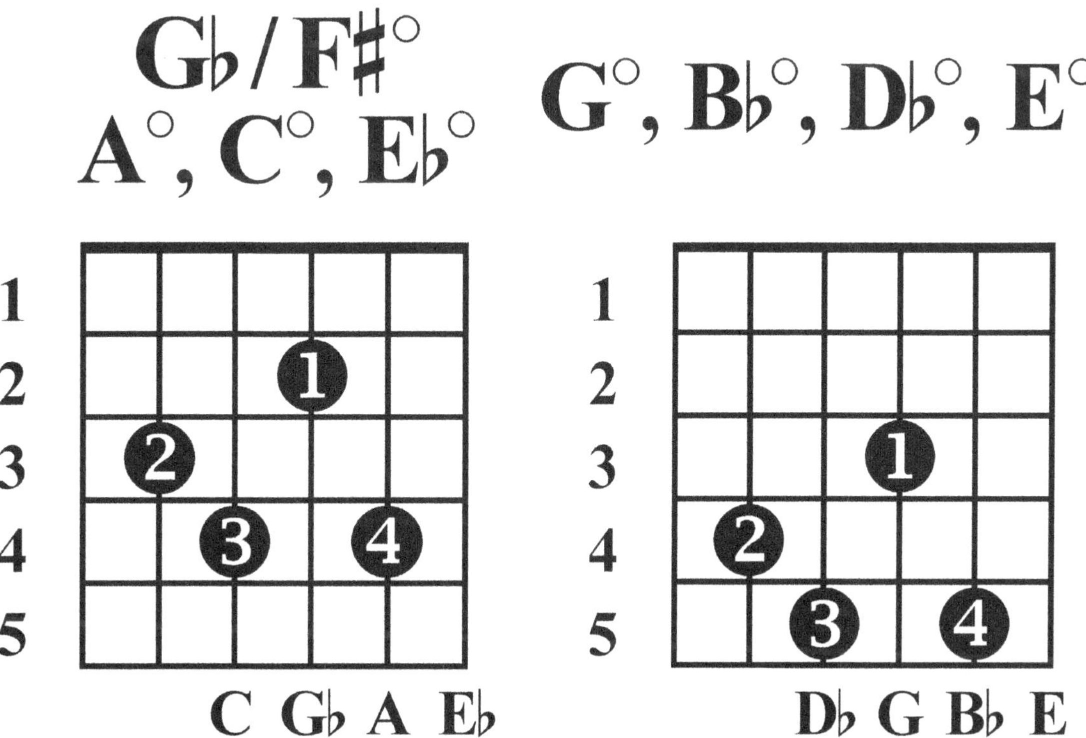

Augmented

F$^+$, C$\sharp$, A$^+$

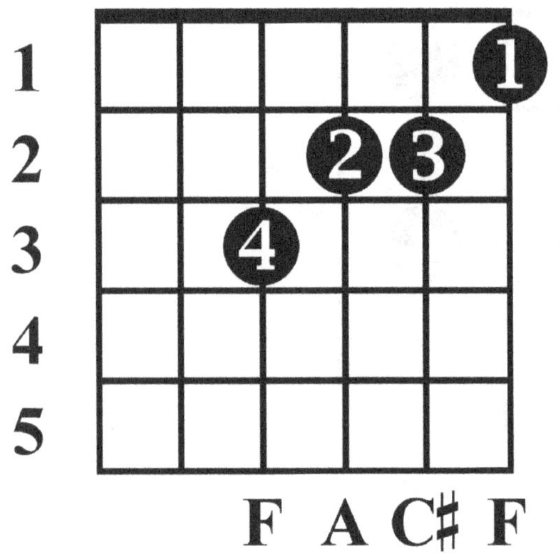

G$\flat$ / F$\sharp$$^+$
D$^+$, B$\flat$$^+$

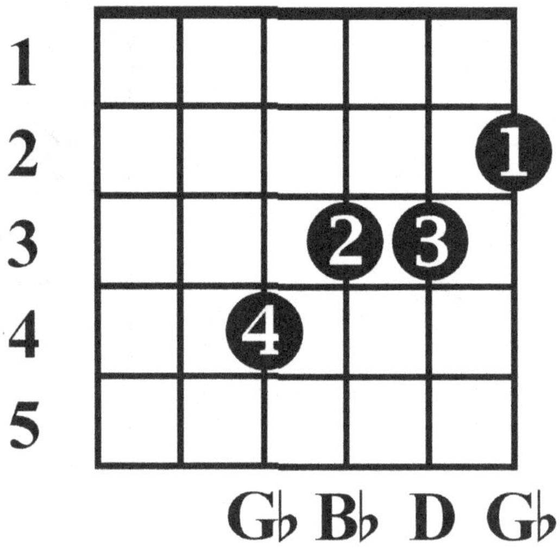

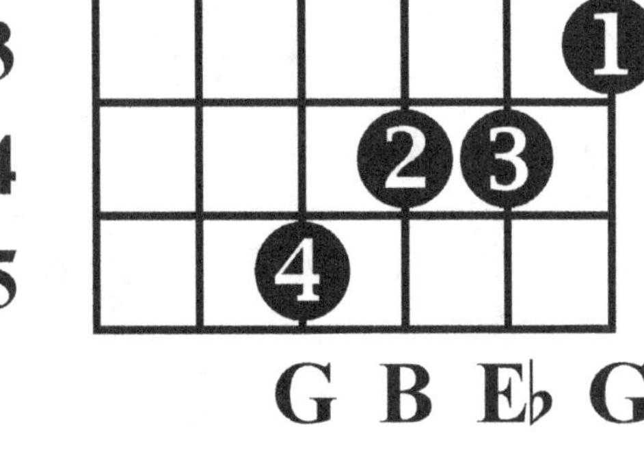

G$^+$, E$\flat$$^+$, B$^+$

A$\flat$$^+$, E$^+$, C$^+$

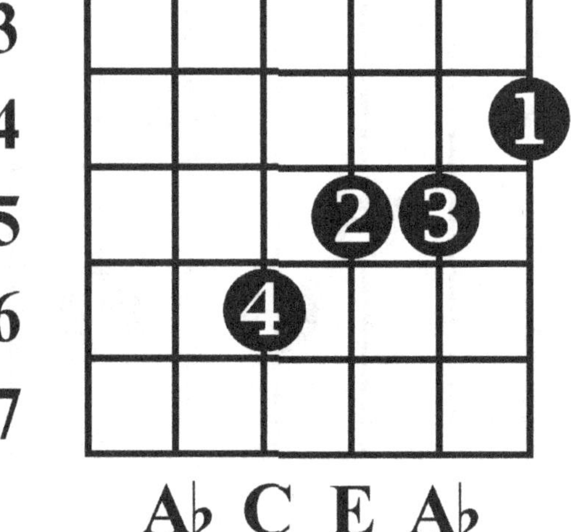

Another Augmented Form

C^+, E^+, $A\flat^+$

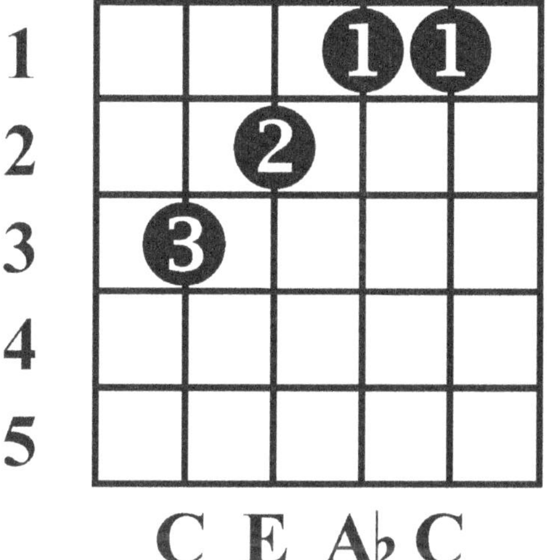

$D\flat^+$, F^+, A^+

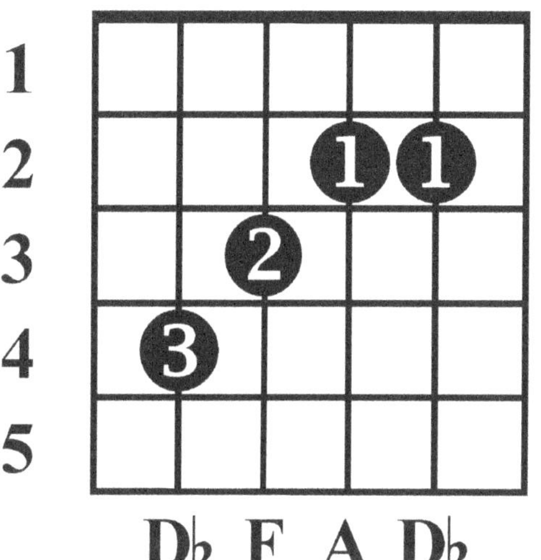

$G\flat$ / $F\sharp^+$ D^+, $B\flat^+$

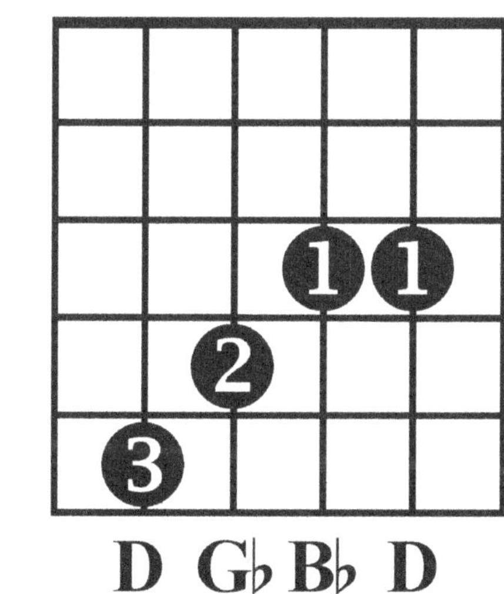

$E\flat^+$, G^+, B^+

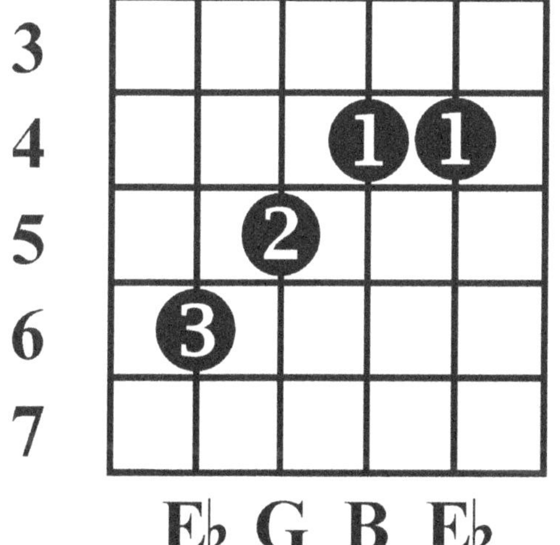

Ready for the next step?

Check out Mel Bay's

Guitar Journals - Chords

by William Bay

- Ultimate guide of chord studies and perfect reference manual for everyday use.
- A comprehensive presentation of modern chord forms with analysis on how to use them effectively in contemporary music.
- Beautiful hard cover with spiral binding.

$24.95 (MB#20905)